ROUTLEDGE LIBRARY EDITIONS:
THE ENGLISH LANGUAGE

Volume 12

THE GRAMMAR OF ENGLISH REFLEXIVES

THE GRAMMAR OF ENGLISH REFLEXIVES

MICHAEL HELKE

LONDON AND NEW YORK

First published in 1979

This edition first published in 2015
by Routledge
2 Park Square, Milton Park, Abingdon, Oxon OX14 4RN

and by Routledge
711 Third Avenue, New York, NY 10017

Routledge is an imprint of the Taylor & Francis Group, an informa business

© 1979 Michael Helke

All rights reserved. No part of this book may be reprinted or reproduced or utilised in any form or by any electronic, mechanical, or other means, now known or hereafter invented, including photocopying and recording, or in any information storage or retrieval system, without permission in writing from the publishers.

Trademark notice: Product or corporate names may be trademarks or registered trademarks, and are used only for identification and explanation without intent to infringe.

British Library Cataloguing in Publication Data
A catalogue record for this book is available from the British Library

ISBN: 978-1-138-92111-5 (Set)
ISBN: 978-1-315-68654-7 (Set) (ebk)
ISBN: 978-1-138-90817-8 (Volume 12) (hbk)
ISBN: 978-1-138-91890-0 (Volume 12) (pbk)
ISBN: 978-1-315-68817-6 (Volume 12) (ebk)

Publisher's Note
The publisher has gone to great lengths to ensure the quality of this reprint but points out that some imperfections in the original copies may be apparent.

Disclaimer
The publisher has made every effort to trace copyright holders and would welcome correspondence from those they have been unable to trace.

The Grammar of English Reflexives

Michael Helke

Garland Publishing, Inc. ■ New York & London
1979

Library of Congress Cataloging in Publication Data

Helke, Michael, 1943–
  The grammar of English reflexives.

  (Outstanding dissertations in linguistics)
  Originally presented as the author's thesis,
Massachusetts Institute of Technology, 1970.
  Bibliography: p.
  1. English language—Pronoun. I. Title. II. Series.
PE1261.H39 1979   425   78-66542
ISBN 0-8240-9684-3

© 1979 Michael Helke
All rights reserved

All volumes in this series are printed on acid-free,
250-year-life paper.
Printed in the United States of America

ACKNOWLEDGEMENTS

Many of my teachers and fellow students have discussed the material presented in this thesis with me. I am particularly grateful to my teachers Noam Chomsky, Kenneth L. Hale, Morris Halle, G. Hubert Matthews, and John Robert Ross for having carefully read my thesis and having given me the benefit of their criticisms. Joan W. Bresnan, Ray C. Dougherty, Barbara Hall Partee, James C. Meadors, John Moyne, and Thomas Wasow have commented on parts of this thesis and have suggested improvements. I am especially grateful to Jean D. Thompson for her help with the manuscript.

TABLE OF CONTENTS

CHAPTER ONE	1
CHAPTER TWO	25
CHAPTER THREE	98
CHAPTER FOUR	155
BIBLIOGRAPHY	174

CHAPTER ONE

It is widely assumed that reflexivization and pronominalization are but two aspects of one and the same syntactic phenomenon. The basis for this assumption is the contention that reflexives are in complementary distribution with anaphoric pronouns. Specifically, the contention is that the conditions under which reflexives are associated with antecedents are just those conditions under which anaphoric pronouns can not be associated with antecedents, and conversely, that the conditions under which reflexives can not be associated with antecedents are just those conditions under which anaphoric pronouns are associated with antecedents. Whatever validity this contention may have for other languages, it is not compatible with the facts of English. Without examining what the conditions are under which pronouns and reflexives are supposedly associated with their antecedents, one can tell that this contention is wrong from a consideration of the two examples (1) and (2).

(1) The young woman took it upon her to head the revolution

(2) The young woman took it upon herself to head the revolution

Sentences (1) and (2) are identical except that (1) has the

anaphoric pronoun her where (2) has the reflexive herself. In
(1) the antecedent of the pronoun is the subject of the sentence
just as in (2) the antecedent of the reflexive is the subject
of that sentence. It follows that the conditions under which
the anaphoric pronoun in (1) is associated with its antecedent
are the same as the conditions under which the reflexive in (2)
is associated with its antecedent. This, of course, contradicts
the contention that anaphoric pronouns and reflexives are in
complementary distribution, and the whole matter could be laid
to rest.

However, in the case of examples similar to (1) and (2) an
analysis has been proposed according to which (1) and (2) would
only be superficially alike and where underlyingly the conditions
under which the anaphoric pronoun in (1) and the reflexive in
(2) are associated with their respective antecedents are not
the same. Essentially identical proposals have been made by
Lees and Klima (1963), Hall (1965), and Chomsky (1965), among
others. Chomsky, to take one example, has argued that the
sentence I kept it near me derives from a structure of the form
I kept it S where in place of the S node a sentential phrase of
the form It is near me is embedded and that the sentence I aimed
it at myself derives from a structure of the form I aimed it at

me with no sentential embeddings. The absence of sentential is accounted for by the fact that there is no well-formed sentence of the form It was at me. This analysis would account for the anaphoric pronoun in the first sentence and the reflexive in the second, and it is plausible in the case of these two examples. As Chomsky himself notes, however, there are examples that seem to conflict with it. For instance, in the case of sentence (1) there is no sentence of the form it was upon her to head the revolution as this analysis would require. What is more, even if this were not so, the proposed analysis would imply that sentences (1) and (2), which are essentially the same, are only superficially alike. Their underlying structures would be radically different. Sentence (1) would derive from a structure involving a sentential embedding while sentence (2) would derive from one that does not. In view of this, the proposed analysis can not be adapted to the case of sentences (1) and (2). But if one is to reject this analysis in this case, then one must be prepared to find another explanation for these sentences.

In looking at examples like (1) and (2) one finds considerable variation from speaker to speaker with regard to the possibility of an anaphoric pronoun and a reflexive being associated with an antecedent noun phrase under the same conditions. In particular cases some speakers allow either a pronoun or a reflexive, others allow only a pronoun, and yet others only a reflexive. It is doubtful, however, that those for whom a particular pair of examples such as (1) and (2) is questionable do not have other examples in the dialects they speak in which a pronoun and a reflexive may alternate. To account for the diversity of dialects on this point, one might choose ad hoc markings in the lexical entry for each of these expressions indicating whether an anaphoric pronoun or a reflexive would be considered acceptable. Such ad hoc markings are quite appropriate in this case, since they reflect the absence of a systematic variation from one dialect to another. This explanation for the facts of sentences like (1) and (2), of course, can also be extended to those cases in which the analysis discussed earlier does not fail.

If one examines the specific conditions under which anaphoric pronouns and reflexives are supposedly associated with their respective antecedents, one finds additional evidence indicating that anaphoric pronouns are not in complementary distribution with reflexives. One can, of course,

avoid the problems that this evidence raises by amending the
conditions in question. It is nevertheless of interest to
look at this evidence. First, however, it is necessary to
clear up some terminology.

Various terms have been introduced to characterize the
distribution of reflexives and their antecedents, on the one
hand, and anaphoric pronouns and their antecedents, on the
other; and it is necessary to add yet another. Two constituents each of which is dominated by every sentential
phrase dominating the other will be said to have the same
sentential ancestry.

The notion <u>same sentential ancestry</u> captures the same
facts as the notion <u>same simplex sentence</u> of Lees and Klima
(1963) and the notion <u>clause mates</u> of Postal (1968a). These
same facts can also be expressed in terms of the notion of
<u>command</u> of Langacker (1966=1969). In view of this prolif-
eration of terminology, some justification for this new term
is called for. In this paper, the term <u>sentential phrase</u> is
used to refer to either a sentence such as <u>The enemy destroyed
the city</u> or to a nominal with the internal structure of a
sentence such as <u>The enemy's destruction of the city</u>. Whenever it is necessary to be precise, a sentence will be called

a sentential phrase with a verbal head, and a nominal with the internal structure of a sentence will be called a sentential phrase with a nominal head. Sentential ancestry is determined with reference to sentential phrases irrespective of whether they have verbal or nominal heads. The notions *simplex sentence*, *clause mates*, and *command*, however, are only defined in relation to sentential phrases with verbal heads. Taking into account only sentential phrases with verbal heads, the sentence The correspondent reported the enemy's destruction of the city must be analyzed as a single sentential phrase. Any two constituents of this sentence, therefore, are in the same simplex sentence in the terminology of Lees and Klima (1963). They are clause mates in the terminology of Postal (1968a), and they command each other in the terminology of Langacker (1966=1969).

Taking into account, however, both sentential phrases with verbal heads and sentential phrases with nominal heads, the same sentence must be analyzed as a sentential phrase with a verbal head of the form The correspondent reported S in which the sentential phrase the enemy's destruction of the city (which has a nominal head) is embedded in place of the S. The entire sentence consists of two sentential phrases one of which is embedded in the other. Every constituent of the embedded phrase is dominated by the matrix phrase as well as by the embedded phrase. Every constituent of the matrix phrase, however, is dominated only by the matrix phrase. Therefore, a constituent of the matrix phrase and a constituent of the embedded phrase can not be said to have the same sentential ancestry. The significance of this difference between the notion same sentential ancestry and the notions it supplants will become clear in Chapters Two and Three. Expressed in terms of sentential ancestry, the specific contention regarding the conditions under which reflexives and anaphoric pronouns occur is this. 1) Reflexives are associated with antecedents that have the same sentential ancestry as they, while 2) anaphoric pronouns are not associated with antecedents that have the same sentential ancestry as they. Conversely, 3) reflexives are not associated with antecedents that do not have the same sentential ancestry as they, while 4) anaphoric pronouns are associated with antecedents that do not have the same sentential ancestry as they. This distribution of reflexives and their antecedents, on the one hand, and of anaphoric pronouns and their antecedents, on the other, can be illustrated by sentences such as (3)-(6).

(3) The old man will help himself

(4) The old man will help him

(5) The shepherd boy hopes the old man will help himself

(6) The shepherd boy hopes the old man will help him

In sentence (3) the subject noun phrase the old man is associated with the reflexive object himself as its antecedent. Since the subject and the object of any sentence are of the same sentential ancestry, this shows that reflexives are associated with antecedents that have the same sentential ancestry as they have. In sentence (4), on the other hand, the subject noun phrase the old man can not be associated with the object pronoun him. This shows that anaphoric pronouns are not associated with antecedents that have the same sentential ancestry as they. Sentence (5) consists of a matrix sentence The shepherd boy hopes S in which the sentential The old man will help himself is embedded in place of the S. The embedded sentential phrase is identical to sentence (3) and, as in the case of (3), the subject noun phrase the old man is associated with the reflexive object himself as its antecedent. The noun phrase the shepherd boy in the subject

of the matrix sentence, however, can not be associated with
the reflexive himself in the object of the embedded sentential
phrase as its antecedent. Since the embedded sentential phrase
is an ancestor of the reflexive but not of the subject of the
matrix, this shows that reflexives are not associated with
antecedents that do not have the same sentential ancestry as
they. Sentence (6) consists of the same matrix as sentence (5),
The shepherd boy hopes S, in which the sentential phrase The
old man will help him is embedded in place of the S. The embedded sentnetial phrase is identical to sentence (4), and,
as in the case of (4), the subject noun phrase the old man can
not be associated with the object pronoun him as its antecedent.
The noun phrase the shepherd boy in the subject of the matrix
sentence, however, can be associated with the pronoun him in
the object of the embedded sentential phrase as its antecedent.
Since the embedded sentential phrase is an ancestor of the
pronoun but not of the subject of the matrix, this shows that
anaphoric pronouns are associated with antecedents that do
not have the same sentential ancestry as they.

Sentences like (3)-(6) are consistent with the contention
that reflexives are associated with antecedents that have the
same sentential ancestry as they. (Why this is so will be

shown in Chapter Two.) They are also consistent with the claim that reflexives are not associated with antecedents that do not have the same sentential ancestry as they. (A number of apparent counter-examples to this will be taken up in Chapter Three.) Indeed, sentences (3)-(6) are consistent with the claim that anaphoric pronouns are associated with antecedents that do not have the same sentential ancestry as they. Really they are consistent with the contention that anaphoric pronouns are not associated with antecedents that have the same sentential ancestry as they. It is not always the case, however, that anaphoric pronouns are not associated with antecedents that have the same sentential ancestry as they. The anaphoric pronoun in sentence (1) is a case in point. For another instance, pronominal possessive determiners can be associated with appropriate antecedent noun phrases even if both have the same sentential ancestry. Similarly, even when both pronoun and antecedent have the same sentential ancestry, possessive determiners can be associated with appropriate anaphoric pronouns as their antecedents. This is shown by examples like (7) and (8).

  (7) The rich girl loves her husband

  (8) The rich girl's husband loves her

The noun phrase the rich girl in sentence (7) can be associated with the pronoun her in the determiner of the noun phrase her husband as its antecedent, just as in sentence (8) the noun phrase the rich girl in the determiner of the noun phrase the rich girl's husband can be associated with the pronoun her as its antecedent. In either case, the determiner in question is a possessive determiner. In either case, the pronoun and the antecedent with which it is associated appear to have the same sentential ancestry. Hence, sentences (7) and (8) apparently contradict the contention that anaphoric pronouns are not associated with antecedents that have the same sentential ancestry as they. (It is true but irrelevant that the conditions under which the pronouns in (7) and (8) are associated with their respective antecedents do not allow reflexives to be associated with antecedents.) Lees and Klima (1963) have sought to avoid this apparent contradiction by postulating a stage in the derivation of the possessive determiners in which those determiners do not have the same sentential ancestry as the noun phrases with which they are associated or as the pronouns associated with them. In particular, they argue that possessive determiners are derived transformationally from certain embedded sentential phrases. On this analysis, sentence

(7) can at one stage in its derivation be represented as (9) and sentence (8) as (10).

(9) The rich girl loves the husband she has

(10) The husband the rich girl has loves her

The possessive determiner *her* in sentence (7) derives from the subject *she* of the sentential phrase *she has* embedded in (9). This sentential phrase is an ancestor of the pronoun *she* but not of the noun phrase *the rich girl*, which can be associated with this pronoun or the possessive determiner that derives from it as an antecedent. The possessive determiner *the rich girl's* in sentence (8) derives from the subject of the sentential phrase *the rich girl has* which is embedded in (10). This sentential phrase is an ancestor of the noun phrase *the rich girl* but not of the anaphoric pronoun *her* with which this noun phrase can be associated as an antecedent. In this way the analysis of Lees and Klima relates the possibility of associating the noun phrase *the rich girl* in sentence (7) with the pronoun *her* in the determiner of the noun phrase *her husband* to the possibility of associating the same noun phrase in sentence (9) with the pronoun *she* in the subject of the sentential phrase embedded in (9). By the same token, in sentence (8) the analysis of Lees and Klima relates the possibility of associating the noun phrase <u>the rich girl</u> in the determiner of the noun phrase <u>the rich girl's husband</u> with the pronoun <u>her</u> to the possibility of associating the same noun phrase in the subject of the sentential phrase embedded in (10) to the pronoun <u>her</u> in sentence (10). In general, this analysis equates the possibility of associating possessive determiners with other noun phrases and the possibility of associating the subjects of the embedded sentential phrases from which it derives possessive determiners with those other noun phrases. Whenever the subject of the embedded phrase can be associated with a given pronoun as its antecedent, the possessive determiner derived from it can also. Whenever the subject of the embedded phrase can be associated with a given antecedent noun phrase, the possessive determiner derived from it can also. Consider, however, a sentence like (11).

(11) The husband she has loves the rich girl

The noun phrase <u>the rich girl</u> in (11) can be associated with the pronoun <u>she</u> in the subject of the sentential phrase embedded in (11). From the structure underlying sentence (11) one can derive a sentence in which the embedded sentential phrase has been converted into a possessive determiner in accordance with the analysis of Lees and Klima. This sentence is shown in (12).

(12) Her husband loves the rich girl

There is some dispute as to whether or not in a sentence like (12) the object noun phrase (<u>the rich girl</u> in the case of (12)) can be associated with the determiner of the subject (<u>her</u> in this case) as an antecedent. To the extent that this is not possible, the analysis that derives possessive determiners from embedded sentential phrases breaks down. The possibility of associating possessive determiners with other noun phrases can not be related to the possibility of associating the subjects of the embedded sentential phrases from which possessive determiners putatively derive with other noun phrases. The conditions under which the putative sources of possessive determiners enter into such associations are not the same as the conditions under which possessive determiners themselves do. In view of this, the explanation that Lees and Klima give for the apparent contradiction of the claim that anaphoric pronouns are not associated with antecedents that have the same sentential ancestry as they is as controversial as the possibility of associating the noun phrase <u>the rich girl</u> in sentence (12) with the pronominal possessive determiner <u>her</u> as its antecedent.

Alongside of examples (3)-(6) there are certain other

examples that have been interpreted in much the same way. In contrast with examples (3)-(6), however, these examples are not concerned with the possibility of associating reflexives and anaphoric pronouns with appropriate antecedents. They are, therefore, not primarily concerned with the interpretation of sentences. Rather, the examples in question show a certain correspondence between reflexives and first and second person pronouns, on the one hand, and the well-formedness or ill-formedness of certain sentences in which they occupy object position, on the other. In particular, they show that whenever, in a given sentence, a first or second person object pronoun is associated with the equivalent subject pronoun, then the sentence is ill-formed. Corresponding to each of these ill-formed sentences, however, is a well-formed sentence in which an appropriate reflexive takes the place of the object pronoun. Conversely, whenever a reflexive object is not associated with an equivalent subject, the sentence is ill-formed. Again, however, corresponding to each of these ill-formed sentences is a well-formed sentence in which an appropriate personal pronoun takes the place of the reflexive. Sentences (13)-(24) are arranged in two columns so as to illustrate this correspondence between well-formed and ill-formed sentences.

(Sentence (13) goes with sentence (16), etc.)

    (13) *I know me   (16) I know myself

    (14) I know you   (17) *I know yourself

    (15) I know him   (18) *I know himself

    (19) You know me   (22) *You know myself

    (20) *You know you   (23) You know yourself

    (21) You know him   (24) *You know himself

In each case where the sentence in the left-hand column of (13)-(24) is ill-formed, the corresponding sentence in the right-hand column is well-formed; conversely, in each case where the sentence in the left-hand column is well-formed, the corresponding sentence in the right-hand column is ill-formed. This does, indeed, give the appearance that the reflexives in the objects of the sentences in the right-hand column are in complementary distribution with the corresponding pronouns in the object of the sentences in the left-hand column. Halle (1964a, 1964b), Keyser (1964), Keyser and Halle (1968) suggest that this distribution of well-formed and ill-formed sentences shows that the well-formed sentences with reflexive objects should be derived from the structures underlying the ill-formed sentences which have the corresponding pronoun instead of the reflexive. This would be done by an obligatory rule that substitutes the appropriate reflexive for the pronoun. Such a rule would account for the fact that these structures can not show up as well-formed sentences with a pronominal object since it obligatorily converts each of them into the corresponding sentence with a reflexive object. The same rule would also account for the ill-formedness of those reflexive sentences that correspond to well-formed sentences with pronominal objects. This rule, which is the only source of reflexives, simply does not apply to the structures underlying the well-formed sentences with pronominal objects. In effect, it only applies to structures that, but for the fact that it does apply, would yield ill-formed sentences. There are, therefore, no underlying structures to which the reflexive rule might apply to derive the sentences in question, and this accounts for their ill-formedness.

If it were not for the fact that the ill-formedness of sentences with first or second person object pronouns can be related to the ill-formedness of certain other sentences which bear no relation to reflexives and for which there are no corresponding well-formed reflexive sentences, the above considerations would indeed be a competing argument for deriving reflexives from personal pronouns in the way indicated above.

Consider, however, the ill-formedness of sentences (25)-(28).

    (25) *I know me (=13)

    (26) *We know me

    (27) *We know us

    (28) *I know us

Sentence (25), which repeats sentence (13), and sentence (27) could both be accounted for in the way sentence (13) was accounted for above. Both have first person object pronouns associated with the equivalent subject pronoun. Corresponding to each, there is a well-formed sentence in which an appropriate reflexive takes the place of the object pronoun. This, however, is not true of sentences (26) and (28). Both have a first person object pronoun associated with a first person subject pronoun, though not the equivalent subject pronoun. For neither of them is there a corresponding well-formed sentence in which a reflexive takes the place of the object pronoun. Hence, the ill-formedness of (26) and (28) can not be accounted for in the same terms as the ill-formedness of sentences (25) and (27). Indeed, the explanation for the ill-formedness of (26) and (28) is independent of the question of reflexives. Sentences like (26) and (28) are characterized by the fact that they have first or second person object pronouns

that are associated with first or second person subject
pronouns, respectively. Along the lines of sentences (26)
and (28), there are ill-formed sentences in which second
person object pronouns are associated with second person
subject pronouns, though in English these are no different
from the ill-formed sentences in which a second person object
pronoun is associated with the equivalent subject pronoun.
All have the same form as example (20). There are, of course,
no ill-formed sentences with third person object associated
with third person subject unless they are ill-formed for
some independent reason. To account for the ill-formed
sentences with first or second person object pronouns associated
respectively with first or second person subject pronouns, one
might tentatively postulate a universal constraint of which
the following formulation gives a special case. <u>A sentence is
ill-formed whenever is subject and its direct object are either
both first or both second person.</u>[1] This constraint as it is
formulated covers all sentences in which a first or second
person object pronoun is associated (respectively) with a first
or second person subject pronoun, whether it is the equivalent
pronoun, as in the case of (25) and (27), or whether it is not,
as in the case of (26) and (28). This constraint, therefore,

provides an alternative to the approach that relates the
ill-formedness of sentences with first or second person
object pronouns that are associated with equivalent subject
pronouns to the well-formedness of the corresponding sentences
in which the object pronoun has been replaced by an appropriate
reflexive. The alternative explanation that this new approach
provides relates the ill-formedness of these sentences to the
ill-formedness of all sentences with first or second person
object pronouns that are associated (respectively) with first
or second person subject pronouns. The alternative explanation
in effect supplants the original explanation. In view of this,
there is no reason for the original explanation to be retained.
In order to have a reason for retaining it, one would have to
limit the alternative explanation to just those cases to
which the original explanation does not apply. Of course, the
original explanation also took into account the ill-formedness
of those sentences which have reflexive objects that can not
be associated with appropriate subjects. Therefore, if one is
to dispense with it, one will have to provide an alternative
explanation for these facts. Just such an explanation will
be found in Chapter Two.

It is not only true that a sentence whose subject and

direct object agree in person is ill-formed if they are either first or second person, but much the same can be said about nominals that have the internal structure of sentences. In other words, the constraint not only applies to sentential phrases with verbal heads but also to sentential phrases with nominal heads. The nominals in (29)-(32), whose specifier and direct object complement agree in person, show this to be the case.

(29) *my knowledge of me
(30) *our knowledge of me
(31) *our knowledge of us
(32) *my knowledge of us

In view of the ill-formedness of the nominals in (29)-(32), the constraint formulated above in terms appropriate for examples such as (25)-(28) can be reformulated in terms that are somewhat more general. Following a terminological suggestion of Chomsky (1967=1970) to call the determiner of a sentential phrase with a nominal head the specifier of the nominal head, one may call the subject of a sentential phrase with a verbal head the specifier of the verbal head. This allows one to reformulate the constraint in question in the following way. A sentential phrase is ill-formed whenever the specifier of its

<u>head and its direct object complement are either both first person or both second person</u>. This takes account of the ill-formedness of the sentential phrases in (29)-(32) in each of which the specifier of the nominal head and the direct object complement are either both first or both second person. Furthermore, given the fact that the subject of a sentence is the same thing as the specifier of the head of a sentential phrase with a verbal head, this formulation of the constraint includes the earlier formulation as a special case.

NOTES

1. Postal (1966a) (p. 91, n.1) already recognized that such a constraint is needed and that it probably has the status of a linguistic universal. Speaking of "sentences with subjects and objects which, while not fully identical, embody common reference to either a first or a second person element, i.e. sentences which express meanings like 'I like us', 'we like me', 'we inclusive like you', etc.", he says: "It is interesting that in both Mohawk and English it is apparently impossible to find grammatical sentences which express such meanings. It therefore seems likely that this fact is a universal to be reflected in the theory of grammar rather than an ad hoc fact to be stated in particular descriptions . . ." (For the evidence from Mohawk, see Postal (1962, 1964a).)

Another way of accounting for the ill-formedness of sentences (25)-(28) and other similar sentences is suggested by the Inclusion Constraint of Postal (1968a). The intent of this constraint seems to be the following. A sentence is ill-formed whenever it contains two noun phrases with the same sentential ancestry which have partially or fully the same reference. This would account for the ill-formedness of sentences (25)- (28) because in all of these sentences the subject and the object noun phrases refer to the speaker (of these sentences). Of course, in (26) and (27) the subject noun phrase and in (27) and (28) the object noun phrase refer to other persons as well. The Inclusion Constraint allows one, furthermore, to relate these facts to the supposed fact that the subject and the object noun phrases of a given sentence can never be interpreted as having partially or fully the same reference, even in the case of sentences with third person subject and object like He knows him which are not ill-formed. One can see that this constraint must not apply to sentences with reflexive object noun phrases since these are interpreted as having the same reference as the subject noun phrases and yet these sentences are not ill-formed. Such sentences can be exempted easily. One need only point to the fact that their object noun phrases are in a morphological class by themselves. It is not easy, however to see how sentences like Violence begets violence, which to be sure are well-formed, can be exempted from this constraint. In sentences of this kind the subject and object noun phrases have the same reference and yet the object noun phrases are not in an identifiable morphological class by themselves. In view of these considerations this approach must be considered tentative.

CHAPTER TWO

Within the framework of generative grammar the question of English reflexives has been discussed in three important papers: Lees and Klima (1963), Postal (1966b), and Jackendoff (1968), the relevant sections of which are repeated verbatim in Jackendoff (1969). Lees and Klima (1963) derive a reflexive by transformationally substituting it for one of a pair of noun phrases that meet certain conditions of identity. Lees and Klima do not elaborate on these conditions; their examples, however, show that the underlying representation of the antecedent and the underlying representation of the reflexive must at least have the same syntactic properties. The derivation of a reflexive is obligatory in the first and second person. In the third person it is optional because here it is possible for the underlying representations of two noun phrases to meet the requisite conditions of identity and yet for neither to be the antecedent of the other. The usual example of this is a sentence like John hates John in which the two occurrences of the noun phrase John are 'identical' and also satisfy the other conditions that would allow one to substitute a reflexive for one.

Postal (1966b) imposes the same conditions on the underlying structure of a reflexive and its antecedent. In addition, however, he requires that the underlying representation of a reflexive and the underlying representation of the antecedent be marked for identity of reference. If a given pair of noun phrases is not so marked, then one can not substitute a reflexive for one even if the underlying representations of the noun phrases in question have the same syntactic properties. By adding to the conditions of identity which a pair of noun phrases must meet in order for a reflexive to be substituted for one the requirement that they be marked for identity of reference, Postal (1966b) can make the reflexivization process obligatory. Where a pair of noun phrases that has the same syntactic properties and that also satisfies the other conditions that would allow a reflexive to be substituted for one does not undergo reflexivization, this can be accounted for by the assumption that they were not marked for identity of reference.

In spite of their differences, the approach to the question of reflexives of Lees and Klima (1963) and that of Postal (1966b) may be considered two different formulations of one and the same theory of reflexivization. Reflexives as such are not present in the deep structure. A given surface structure reflexive derives transformationally from an underlying noun phrase which meets certain conditions of identity with respect to some other noun phrase, its antecedent. The identity condition stipulates at least that the head of the underlying representation of a reflexive and the head of the underlying representation of its antecedent have the same syntactic properties. Call this the transformational theory of reflexivization.

Jackendoff (1969) considers his approach to reflexivization an alternative to the transformational theory of reflexivization which he calls 'the standard generative grammar approach.' In fact, he claims that the difference between his approach and that of the transformational theory is 'fundamental'. In point of fact, however, Jackendoff's approach can conceivably be interpreted as a notational variant of the transformational theory of reflexivization. While it is true that his approach differs from the usual formulations of the transformation theory in that reflexives are in his approach not derived transformationally, this difference is of no empirical consequence. According to Jackendoff, reflexives are lexical items. Like all lexical items they are inserted at the level of deep structure. A rule of interpretation associates reflexives with potential grammatical antecedents, where a potential grammatical antecedent is any noun phrase that can

be the antecedent of some reflexive. As a result of this
operation, reflexives and antecedents may or may not be
properly matched. If reflexive and antecedent are properly
matched, as in a sentence like John washed himself, nothing
must be added. If they are not properly matched, however,
as in the sentence John washed yourself, and if, furthermore,
they can not be properly matched, then the structure concerned
must be excluded. To do this, Jackendoff imposes an identity
condition which reflexives and their antecedents must meet.
He describes this condition as 'the obvious general convention
that coreferential noun phrases must be able to have the same
reference and thus must agree in number, person, and gender
as well as animacy, humanness, abstractness, and myriad other
semantic properties'. (Jackendoff (1969), p. 45) The statement that coreferential noun phrases must be able to have the
same reference is not a general convention but a tautology.
Hence, the above quotation reduces to the claim that coreferential noun phrases must agree in number, person, gender, as well
as animacy, humanness, abstractness, and other semantic features,
though not in their phonological properties. Though other interpretations are also possible, one may interpret this as
stipulating that a reflexive and its antecedent must have the

same syntactic properties. This, of course, would be the very
identity condition that characterizes the transformational
theory of reflexivization. Hence, if this is the proper interpretation of Jackendoff's identity condition, then on his
analysis the well-formedness of sentences containing reflexives
is determined by the same condition as in the case of the usual
formulations of the transformational theory. On this interpretation, the only difference between Jackendoff's formulation
of this theory and the usual formulations would be that in his
formulation reflexives are not derived transformationally,
though in the other formulations they are. Of course, Jackendoff's identity condition is open to other interpretations, in
particular, one in which a reflexive and its antecedent need
not agree in all syntactic and semantic properties. It seems
certain that in stating this condition, Jackendoff was only
hand-waving, but hand-waving is not appropriate at this point.
Jackendoff depends on this condition to account for the ill-formedness of sentences in which a reflexive can not be matched
up with an appropriate antecedent. Hence, he should have
demonstrated that this condition can both account for these
sentences and avoid the consequences of the identity condition
of the transformational theory of reflexivization. If his theory

of reflexivization can not handle sentences in which reflexives can not be associated with appropriate antecedents, then it is observationally inadequate. If it can handle such sentences only by imposing the same identity conditions that the transformational theory of reflexivization imposes, then this theory is only a notational variant of the transformational theory.

This chapter will argue for a true alternative to the transformational theory of reflexivization. This alternative theory, called the phrase structure of reflexivization, analyzes English reflexives as members of a certain subset of possessives, for which the term "restricted possessives" will be used. According to this conception of reflexivization, reflexives are represented in the deep structure as possessives with the head noun <u>self</u>. Consequently, the underlying representation of a reflexive and that of its antecedent need not have the same syntactic properties. In fact, they would have the same properties only when the antecedent happened to have the syntactic properties of the noun <u>self</u>. Inasmuch as the identity condition imposed by the transformational theory has empirical content, the transformational and the phrase structure theories of reflexivization are distinguishable in terms of the competing claims they make with respect to this condition.

same syntactic properties. This, of course, would be the very identity condition that characterizes the transformational theory of reflexivization. Hence, if this is the proper interpretation of Jackendoff's identity condition, then on his analysis the well-formedness of sentences containing reflexives is determined by the same condition as in the case of the usual formulations of the transformational theory. On this interpretation, the only difference between Jackendoff's formulation of this theory and the usual formulations would be that in his formulation reflexives are not derived transformationally, though in the other formulations they are. Of course, Jackendoff's identity condition is open to other interpretations, in particular, one in which a reflexive and its antecedent need not agree in all syntactic and semantic properties. It seems certain that in stating this condition, Jackendoff was only hand-waving, but hand-waving is not appropriate at this point. Jackendoff depends on this condition to account for the ill-formedness of sentences in which a reflexive can not be matched up with an appropriate antecedent. Hence, he should have demonstrated that this condition can both account for these sentences and avoid the consequences of the identity condition of the transformational theory of reflexivization. If his theory of reflexivization can not handle sentences in which reflexives can not be associated with appropriate antecedents, then it is observationally inadequate. If it can handle such sentences only by imposing the same identity conditions that the transformational theory of reflexivization imposes, then this theory is only a notational variant of the transformational theory.

This chapter will argue for a true alternative to the transformational theory of reflexivization. This alternative theory, called the phrase structure of reflexivization, analyzes English reflexives as members of a certain subset of possessives, for which the term "restricted possessives" will be used. According to this conception of reflexivization, reflexives are represented in the deep structure as possessives with the head noun <u>self</u>. Consequently, the underlying representation of a reflexive and that of its antecedent need not have the same syntactic properties. In fact, they would have the same properties only when the antecedent happened to have the syntactic properties of the noun <u>self</u>. Inasmuch as the identity condition imposed by the transformational theory has empirical content, the transformational and the phrase structure theories of reflexivization are distinguishable in terms of the competing claims they make with respect to this condition.

This chapter develops an argument to choose between these two theories. It is based on the following considerations. To a considerable extent the syntax of English reflexives can be accounted for by either the transformational or the phrase structure theory of reflexivization. While the transformational theory is motivated by the facts about reflexives alone and does not generalize to other syntactic phenomena, the phrase structure theory is motivated by the facts about restricted possessives, quite independently of reflexives. In view of this the transformational theory would appear superfluous. By analyzing reflexives as restricted possessives, which the grammar of English must account for irrespective of the question of reflexives, the phrase structure theory can account for their syntax at no added cost. What is more, to the extent that the transformational and the phrase structure theories differ with respect to the syntactic distribution they predict, the facts of English accord with the prediction of the phrase structure theory.

By way of introduction it is necessary to make some rather general remarks concerning the relation between anaphoric pronouns and their antecedents. Thus, in general the syntactic well-formedness of a sentence (throughout the term <u>well-formedness</u>, unless qualified, is to be understood as meaning syntactic well-formedness) does not depend on the possibility of associating an appropriate antecedent with any given pronoun. The well-formedness of a sentence like <u>He sings in the shower</u>, where no possible antecedent for the pronoun <u>he</u> is present, illustrates this. The same point can be made with regard to sentences containing pronouns that can possibly be associated with appropriate antecedents. Insofar as the well-formedness of such sentences does not depend on this possibility, it is not affected when the antecedent noun phrases are replaced by otherwise suitable noun phrases that can not be associated with these pronouns as their antecedents. For instance, in the sentence <u>The girl said that she was lonely</u>, the noun phrase <u>the girl</u> may be interpreted as the antecedent of the pronoun <u>she</u>. The possibility of associating the pronoun with an antecedent does not affect the well-formedness of this sentence. Though putting the noun phrase <u>the girl</u> into the plural makes it impossible to associate it with the pronoun <u>she</u> as its antecedent, this does not cause ill-formedness. On the contrary, it yields the well-formed sentence <u>The girls said that she was lonely</u>. While in general the relation of anaphoric pronouns to their antecedents does not determine the well-formedness of a sentence, there are instances where this is so. For example, the possibility of associating appropriate antecedents with the pronominal determiners of the possessives in (1)-(4) is a precondition on the well-formedness of these sentences:

    (1) The poor girl lost her mind
    (2) We nodded our heads
    (3) The members of the committee expressed their support for the motion
    (4) I blinked my eyes

If the antecedents of these pronouns are eliminated by replacing the antecedent noun phrases with other suitable noun phrases that can not be associated with them as antecedents, ill-formedness results. If, for example, one alters the grammatical number of the antecedents, one obtains the ill-formed structures exhibited in (5)-(8).

    (5) *The poor girls lost her mind
    (6) *I nodded our heads
    (7) *Each member of the committee expressed their support for the motion
    (8) *We blinked my eyes

The ill-formedness of (5)-(8) serves to illustrate the fact that the well-formedness of sentences (1)-(4) is partially determined by the fact that the pronominal possessive determiners in (1)-(4) can be associated with appropriate antecedents.

In order to express the fact that they do not occur freely, this study will call <u>bound</u> those anaphoric pronouns that require antecedents (in the sense that the possibility of associating them with appropriate antecedents is a precondition on the well-formedness of the structures containing them). Since pronouns which are bound are always anaphoric, they will, where it is not necessary to be explicit, simply be called <u>bound pronouns</u>. In addition to the usual conditions on anaphora which for any two noun phrases specify whether one is an antecedent of the other, bound pronouns and their antecedents must satisfy certain other conditions that distinguish them in relation to their antecedents from that of ordinary free anaphoric pronouns in relation to theirs. The requirement that bound pronouns must have antecedents which are appropriate within the relatively broad limits set by the usual conditions on anaphora is only one of these additional conditions. (It goes without saying that in the case of deleted complement and imperative subjects and in similar instances of transformational deletion the required antecedent may not be evident in the surface structure.) A number of other conditions will be mentioned later on in this chapter.

That each bound pronoun is associated with an appropriate antecedent can be ensured if the pronoun is derived from its antecedent as a copy. A copying procedure allows one to account for the well-formedness of (1)-(4) as contrasted with the ill-formedness of (5)-(8) in the following way. In the deep structure the determiners of the possessives are left unspecified (except for the specification that they are possessive determiners). The copying procedure later substitutes a bound pronoun for these determiners. In this way one generates sentences (1)-(4) with the appropriate possessive determiners. On the other hand, sentences (5)-(8) can not be generated because in these sentences the determiners of the possessives have no source.

There are a number of ways in which this proposal can be implemented. For instance, a copying transformation could reproduce the antecedent in full and then submit its output to pronominalization. Certain general conditions on the operation of transformations would have the effect of imposing suitable restrictions on the relation of the copies to their sources reflecting (in a way to be shown later in this chapter) the additional conditions that specifically characterize the relation of bound pronouns to their antecedents. The subsequent derivation of the pronominal forms by the ordinary pronominalization process would account for the properties that are characteristic of all anaphoric pronouns and their antecedents such as the relative linear order of pronouns and antecedents and the morphological shape of the pronouns. One can easily imagine equivalent procedures to derive bound pronouns. For instance, if at some stage of their derivation pronouns are represented as determiners, as Postal (1966b) has suggested, then bound pronouns could be derived by copying the determiners of their antecedents at the appropriate stage, obviating the need for subsequent pronominalization. Since the operation of any copying transformation is governed by certain general conditions that have the effect of imposing suitable restrictions on the relation of the constituents it copies to the copies it yields, the operation of this copying transformation would also reflect the conditions that characterize the relation between bound anaphoric pronouns and their antecedents. As long as the derivation of bound pronouns involves the copying of a portion of their antecedents, the actual formulation of the procedure that does this does not materially affect the discussion in this chapter.

Such a copying procedure, whatever its proper formulation,

is not restricted to copying subject pronouns as in examples
(1)-(4). Consider, for instance, sentence (9).

(9) The rich man met the poor girl on her way home

The well-formedness of sentence (9) depends on the possibility
of associating an appropriate antecedent with the pronoun her
in the determiner of the possessive noun phrase her way home.
The antecedent is in this case the object noun phrase the poor
girl. Substituting for it a suitable noun phrase that is not
an appropriate antecedent for the determiner of the possessive,
one obtains an ill-formed sentence like (10), for example.

(10) *The rich man met the poor girls on her way home

The fact that the pronominal determiner of the possessive in
sentence (9) must be associated with an appropriate antecedent
shows that it is a bound anaphoric pronoun and that the kind
of copying procedure under consideration is the appropriate
device to derive it.

There are similar examples in which both the subject noun
phrase and the object noun phrase are appropriate antecedents
for the bound pronoun in the determiner of the possessive.
Sentence (11) is an example of this kind and, as one can see,
it is possible in this sentence to associate this pronoun with
either antecedent.

(11) The rich girl met the poor girl on her way home

There are other examples where the antecedent of a bound anaphoric pronoun must be either a subject or an object noun phrase even where in other respects both of them are appropriate antecedents. For example, in the sentence The rich girl took the poor girl at her word, the possessive her word is a restricted possessive. Both the subject noun phrase the rich girl and the object noun phrase the poor girl are appropriate antecedents of the anaphoric pronoun her in the determiner of the possessive. In this sentence, however, it is not possible to associate the subject noun phrase with this pronoun as its antecedent. Instead, only the object pronoun can be associated with it as its antecedent. Much the same can be said for the sentence The rich girl gave the poor girl her word. Both subject and object noun phrases are appropriate antecedents for the pronominal determiner of the possessive noun phrase her word. In this case, however, it is not possible to associate the object noun phrase with the pronoun in question as its antecedent. Instead, it takes the subject noun phrase as its antecedent.

It has already been said that bound anaphoric pronouns and their antecedents are set apart from free anaphoric pronouns and their antecedents because they must satisfy certain conditions that free anaphoric pronouns and their antecedents need not satisfy. One of these conditions has to do with the nodes dominating reflexives and the antecedents with which they are associated. It is obvious that there is at least one node dominating any pair of nodes that are part of the same structure, if neither of them dominates the other. In particular, this is true of two noun phrases, one of which is an antecedent of the other. Though in general there are no conditions on the nodes dominating a given noun phrase and the antecedent noun phrase with which it is associated (at least not as long as the antecedent is to the left of the pronoun), bound anaphoric pronouns and their antecedents must indeed satisfy such a condition. The ill-formedness of (9) reflects a violation of this condition.

(12) *The young woman hopes that the poor man won't lose her mind

Given the usual assumptions about sentential structure, the structure underlying the sentential phrase embedded in (9) can be represented informally as The poor man won't lose her mind. The bound pronoun her in (12) is a constituent of the embedded sentential phrase as well as of the matrix sentence. The subject

of the matrix sentence the young woman is a constituent of
that sentence alone. (The subject of the embedded sentential
phrase the poor man can be excluded from consideration because
it is not an appropriate antecedent of the bound pronoun under
any conditions.) The sentence The young woman hopes that the
poor man won't lose her dog duplicates the syntactic conditions
of (12) excepting that the pronoun is not bound. One can see
that under these syntactic conditions the noun phrase the young
woman can be associated with a free but not a bound occurrence
of the anaphoric pronoun her as its antecedent. It follows that
the ill-formedness of (12) is evidence of a condition on bound
anaphoric pronouns and their antecedents, which ordinary free
anaphoric pronouns and their antecedents need not satisfy.
Example (12) shows that it is not possible to associate a bound
pronoun with an antecedent that is not a constituent of every
sentential phrase containing the bound pronoun. But this is
only one aspect of the condition on the nodes dominating bound
pronouns and their antecedents that is under consideration here.
Another aspect of this condition is illustrated by the ill-
formedness of example (13).

(13) *The man who found the poor girl lost her mind
This sentence may, on the usual assumptions about sentential

structure, be analyzed as a matrix sentence of the form The man
S lost her mind with the relative clause who found the poor
girl embedded in place of S. The noun phrase the poor girl is
a constituent of the embedded sentential phrase as well as a
constituent of the matrix sentence. The bound pronoun her, on
the other hand, is a constituent of the matrix sentence alone.
The noun phrase the poor girl can not be associated with the
bound anaphoric pronoun her as its antecedent, though under the
same syntactic conditions it could be associated with a free
occurrence of the same pronoun as an antecedent. One can see
this in a sentence like The man who found the poor girl lost
her purse which duplicates the syntactic conditions of (13)
except for the fact that it has a free anaphoric pronoun in
place of the bound anaphoric pronoun in (13). Sentence (13)
itself is ill-formed because it is not possible to associate
the bound anaphoric pronoun in it with an appropriate antecedent.

Example (13) shows that it is not possible to associate a
bound pronoun with an antecedent that is a constituent of a
sentential phrase that does not contain the bound pronoun. The
earlier example (9) showed that it is not possible to associate
a bound pronoun with an antecedent that is not a constituent of
a sentential phrase that contains the bound pronoun. In other

words, a bound pronoun must be contained in each sentential phrase that contains its antecedent and its antecedent must be contained in each sentential phrase that contains the pronoun. From this it follows that every sentential phrase containing one must also contain the other. A given pair of constituents that meet this condition will be said to have the same sentential ancestry.

The transformational copying procedure postulated as a source for bound pronouns allows one to relate this condition on the sentential ancestry of bound anaphoric pronouns and their antecedents to a more general condition formulated by Chomsky (1965). Chomsky's condition which will be called the insertion prohibition stipulates "that no morphological material . . . can be introduced into a configuration dominated by S once the cycle of transformational rules has already completed its application to this configuration . . ." Together with other conditions, this condition restricts the operation of the copying procedure which introduces bound pronouns in such a way that these pronouns and their antecedents satisfy the condition on their sentential ancestry. No special restrictions need be imposed on the copying procedure. Because of the insertion prohibition, the copying procedure, when applying to a particular sentential phrase S_o, can not cause a bound pronoun to be inserted into a sentential phrase which is embedded in S_o. The cycle of transformational rules will already have applied to such a phrase. In this way, the insertion prohibition explains why the copied constituent from which a bound pronoun derives can not be in a sentential phrase which is embedded in the phrase that contains the constituent that is copied.

The fact that the constituent that is copied, the antecedent, can not be in a sentential phrase which is embedded in the phrase to which the copying procedure applies might be explained by a generalization that was stated by Ross (1967): "Any rule whose structural index is of the form . . . A Y, and whose structural change specifies that A is to be adjoined to the right of Y, is upward bounded." The transformational process that produces bound pronouns has the effect of moving a copy of a constituent A that is followed by a string of variable length Y to the other side of Y. Inasmuch as it is possible to analyze this procedure in such a way that it is not exempt from Ross' generalization because it leaves the constituent copied intact, Ross' generalization would apply. This would have the effect of imposing the appropriate restriction on the operation of this procedure since for a rule to be upward bounded means that it can not extract a constituent contained in a sentential phrase that is embedded in the phrase to which the procedure applies.

There is a condition on the antecedents of bound anaphoric pronouns stipulating that they may not be possessive determiners and single coordinate conjuncts. This is another condition that must be satisfied by the antecedents of bound anaphoric pronouns, though not by the antecedents of free anaphoric pronouns. For instance, in a sentence like The rich girl's husband wasted her money, the noun phrase the rich girl, which in this case is a possessive determiner, can be associated with the free anaphoric pronoun her as its antecedent. Similarly, in a sentence like The rich girl and the gambler wasted her money, where the noun phrase the rich girl is a single coordinate conjunct, it can be associated with the free occurrence of the pronoun her as its antecedent. In view of this the ill-formedness of (14) and (15), which duplicate the syntactic conditions of these sentences except that the anaphoric pronouns in question are bound, is evidence of further restrictive conditions which the antecedents of bound anaphoric pronouns must satisfy in addition to the conditions which the antecedents of any anaphoric pronoun must satisfy.

(14) *The rich girl's husband lost her mind

(15) *The rich girl and the pauper lost her mind

Though the noun phrase the rich girl, which in (14) is a possessive determiner, is an appropriate antecedent for a free occurrence of the anaphoric pronoun her, it can not in this case be associated with the bound occurrence of that pronoun as its required antecedent. In (14) the condition requiring that bound anaphoric pronouns have antecedents is not satisfied. Similarly, the single coordinate conjunct the rich girl in (15), though in other respects an appropriate antecedent, does not fulfill the function of the required antecedent in this sentence.

There is another condition that requires that the antecedent of a bound pronoun be a constituent. Two or more noun phrases that are not a constituent can not be associated with a bound pronoun as its antecedent. This is another condition that must be satisfied by the antecedents of bound anaphoric pronouns though not by the antecedents of anaphoric pronouns as such. The ill-formedness of (16) is due to a violation of this restriction.

(16) *The rich girl found the friendly gentleman on their way home

The two noun phrases <u>the rich girl</u> and <u>the friendly gentleman</u> are not a constituent in (16). They do not fulfill the function of the required antecedent of the bound occurrence of the pronoun <u>their</u> in this sentence. Under the same syntactic conditions, however, they can be associated with a free occurrence of that pronoun as a valid antecedent, as, for instance, in the sentence <u>The friendly gentleman showed the rich girl their new home</u>. The restriction on the antecedents of bound pronouns that the ill-formedness of (16) reflects is explained by the copying procedure that has been postulated as the source of such pronouns. Like all transformations, the copying transformation that is a part of this procedure operates on constituents. It can not copy two or more noun phrases that are not jointly a single constituent. Hence, it does not allow a sentence like (16) to be generated.

It can be observed that the antecedent of a bound anaphoric pronoun is always to its left, while the antecedent of a free anaphoric pronoun may under certain conditions be to its right as well. This is not evidence for another restrictive condition that is satisfied by bound anaphoric pronouns and their antecedents but not satisfied by free anaphoric pronouns and their antecedents. Rather, when an anaphoric pronoun and its antecedent both have the same sentential ancestry, the antecedent must be to the left of the pronoun with which it is associated. This condition must be satisfied by all anaphoric pronouns whether they are bound or free. It is this condition on the relative linear order of anaphoric pronouns and their antecedents that allows the noun phrase the rich lady to be associated as an antecedent with the pronoun her in the determiner of the possessive her husband in (17) and the object pronoun her in sentence (19), but not with the subject pronoun she in sentence (18) and not with the pronoun her in the determiner of the possessive her husband in (20), (because in (17) and (19) this noun phrase is to the left of the pronoun but not in (18) and (20)).

(17) The rich lady loves her husband

(18) She loves the rich lady's husband

(19) The rich lady's husband loves her

(20) Her husband loves the rich lady

In each of (17)-(20) the anaphoric pronoun is free and does not require an antecedent. Consequently, in sentences (18) and (20) the absence of an appropriate antecedent, in particular, an antecedent that is to the left of the pronoun, does not affect well-formedness. In sentence (21), however, the pronoun her is bound and therefore requires an appropriate antecedent. The fact that there is no noun phrase that satisfies the condition on the relative linear order of anaphoric pronouns and their antecedents causes a violation.

(21) *Her mind was lost by the poor girl

Most of the facts about reflexives discussed below can be accommodated by either the phrase structure or the transformational theory of reflexivization. The mechanisms that the phrase structure theory requires to account for these facts, however, must be a part of any grammar, in particular, one that embodies the transformational theory of reflexivization, because they are motivated by considerations that are independent of the question of reflexives. Hence, a grammar that embodies the transformational theory of reflexivization properly includes the phrase structure theory of reflexivization. The following considerations show this. Take, for instance, such expressions as to crane one's neck in a sentence like (22).

(22) The gentleman craned his neck

The verb crane in this sentence has an object noun phrase consisting of the restricted possessive his neck. The determiner of this possessive is redundant. It is not as such represented in the structure underlying this sentence. Rather, it is subsequently derived by the process by which the determiners of all restricted possessives are derived. The important point about sentence (22) is that the verb to crane takes a restricted possessive with the head noun neck as its unique object. The lexical entry for this verb must indicate that the head of the object noun phrase must be the noun neck. Sentences like (22) must be accounted for by any grammar of English, irrespective of how it treats reflexives. Now consider sentence (23) which is an example of an obligatory reflexive, a sentence whose verb uniquely takes a reflexive object.

(23) The defendent perjured himself

In the phrase structure theory of reflexivization this is another instance of the syntactic phenomenon illustrated by sentence (22) above: A verb taking a restricted possessive with a given head noun, self in this case, as its unique object. To account for examples like (23), a grammar that derives reflexives according to the transformational theory of reflexivization has no recourse to this device, even though it does contain the syntactic mechanisms required. On the assumptions of the transformational theory, the underlying representation

of a reflexive and its antecedent must meet certain conditions
of identity. Consequently, if a particular verb requires a
reflexive object the antecedent of which must be the subject
of the sentence in question, then in the underlying structure
this verb must allow as many different objects as it can have
subjects. To account for the fact that in sentences like (23)
the object is always a reflexive that has the subject as its
antecedent, this theory must ensure that the subject and the
object of these sentences always satisfy the conditions of
identity that characterize it. To this end, it has been proposed that in these sentences the object be derived from the
subject by a copying rule. This rule would only apply in the
case of obligatory reflexives, and it does not generalize to
any other cases. The output of this rule is subsequently submitted to reflexivization. Insofar as it accounts for obligatory
reflexives, there is nothing wrong with this analysis. The fact,
however, that the analysis which the phrase structure theory
imposes on obligatory reflexives is available in a grammar that
embodies the transformational theory of reflexivization makes
this analysis superfluous.

Turning to productive cases one can observe that reflexives
and their antecedents satisfy the same conditions that bound

anaphoric pronouns and their antecedents do. Well-formedness requires that each reflexive be associated with an appropriate antecedent. The reflexive and its antecedent must have the same sentential ancestry. The antecedent may not be a possessive determiner or single coordinate conjunct. The antecedent must be a constituent and it must be to the left of the reflexive with which it is associated. In the paragraphs to follow, these properties of reflexives and their antecedents will be examined one by one, and it will be shown how in each case the transformational and the phrase structure theories of reflexivization can account for them.

As in the case of bound pronouns, consideration of well-formedness require that every reflexive be associated with an appropriate antecedent. For instance, in sentence (24) the noun phrase <u>the poor girl</u> is the antecedent of the reflexive <u>herself</u>.

(24) The poor girl hurt herself

If one eliminates from a sentence containing a reflexive any noun phrase that might serve as its antecedent, one obtains an ill-formed structure. In the particular case of sentence (24), if one eliminates the antecedent of the reflexive by putting it into the plural, then one obtains the ill-formed sentence given in (25).

(25) *The poor girls hurt herself

In sentence (25) there is no noun phrase that can be associated with the reflexive as its antecedent. Thus, the ill-formedness of this example shows that the well-formedness of sentences containing reflexives depends on the possibility of associating them with appropriate antecedents. The requirement that each reflexive be associated with an appropriate antecedent can be accounted for in the following ways.

In the transformational approach to reflexivization, reflexives are not present in the deep structure. The transformational process by which they are derived applies to a pair of noun phrases that meet certain conditions of identity with respect to each other. One of these, the antecedent, is left unchanged. For the other, an appropriate reflexive is substituted. In the absence of a suitable pair of noun phrases, no reflexive is derived. The phrase structure theory of reflexivization, on the other hand, interprets the requirement that every reflexive be associated with an appropriate antecedent as a condition on the bound pronoun in the determiner of a restricted possessive and the antecedent of that pronoun. Reflexives, on this analysis, are represented as restricted

possessives. Their head is <u>self</u> and in the deep structure
their determiner is unspecified (except for the specification
that it be a possessive determiner). Subsequently, a copying
procedure substitutes a bound pronoun for this unspecified
determiner. On this analysis the antecedent associated with
a given reflexive is, strictly speaking, the antecedent of
the bound pronoun that is the determiner of the reflexive.
This pronoun is necessarily associated with an appropriate
antecedent by virtue of the copying procedure that derives it
from its antecedent. In the absence of an antecedent, the
unspecified determiner which appears in the underlying representation of a reflexive remains unspecified, eventually
causing the entire structure to be rejected.

In effect, this analysis equates the syntax of a sentence
like <u>The poor girl lost her mind</u> (=1) and the syntax of the
sentence <u>The poor girl hurt herself</u> (=24). One might object
to this by pointing out that sentences such as (1) are stressed
like the sentence <u>The poor girl lost the ráce</u> with main stress
on the object while sentences such as (24) are stressed like
the sentence <u>The poor girl hurt him</u> with main stress on the
verb, and that in general restricted possessives (excluding reflexives) are stressed like fully specified noun phrases while

reflexives are stressed like pronouns. Viewed in their proper perspective these observations do not set reflexives apart from restricted possessives as such. Not only reflexives are stressed like pronouns but, as Chomsky (1955) points out, under certain conditions such fully specified noun phrases as *people* are. Just as the stress profile of the sentence *The poor girl lost the race* contrasts with the stress profile of the sentence *The poor girl hurt him*, so the stress profile of *Hard work matures the mind* and *Adversity strengthens the character*, contrasts with the stress profile of *Hard work matures people* and *Adversity strengthens people*. Whatever the property that pronouns, reflexives, and nouns like *people* under the conditions illustrated by these examples have in common and that sets them apart from other noun phrases that do not have this property, this property happens to cut across the set of restricted possessives in such a way that it isolates reflexives. This distinction which cuts across the entire set of noun phrases does not constitute an objection to the claim that reflexives are restricted possessives.

Incidentally, the phrase structure theory of reflexives readily accounts for the fact that reflexives have their main stress on their final syllable or what on this analysis is their head noun rather than on their initial syllable, as one would expect if they had no internal structure. Since noun phrase determiners in English are generally proclitic, the main stress of a reflexive must be on its head noun. The position of stress in reflexives follows from general facts about the position of stress in noun phrases. It is not given as an inherent property of English reflexives, as Barbara Strang (1962) would have it.

Certain other facts that might be interpreted as conflicting with the analysis that the phrase structure theory of reflexivization imposes on reflexives will be examined at the end of this chapter.

In the example of sentence (24) it was the subject noun phrase that was associated with the reflexive as its antecedent, and for many languages, such as German for example, this is the rule with reflexives. English reflexives, however, may also be associated with antecedent noun phrases that are not in subject position, as one can see in example (26).

(26) The rich man talked to the poor girl about herself

The noun phrase the poor girl which is the antecedent of the reflexive herself in the about phrase in sentence (26) is a prepositional object and not a subject. The possibility of associating a reflexive with an antecedent that is not a subject noun phrase does not pose any problems for the transformational theory of reflexivization. Indeed, to restrict the antecedents of reflexives to subject noun phrases one would have to impose additional conditions on the reflexivization procedure as conceived by this theory. Nor does the possibility of having antecedents that are not subject noun phrases associated with reflexives pose any problems for the phrase structure theory of reflexivization. On the assumptions of this theory, the antecedent of a reflexive is, strictly speaking, the antecedent of the determiner of a restricted possessive with the head noun <u>self</u>. That the antecedent of the determiner of a restricted possessive need not be a subject noun phrase was shown by examples like <u>The rich man met the poor girl on her way home</u>(=9). It is, however, not the case that, as example (26) might suggest, the antecedent of a reflexive must be the first noun phrase to its left. This can be seen in an example like (27) which has a reflexive that is associated with the subject noun phrase and not the prepositional object.

(27) The rich man talked with the poor girl about himself

Inasmuch as it is possible to associate a reflexive in the
about phrase with an antecedent noun phrase in the prepositional
object or with an antecedent noun phrase in subject position,
it is possible to construct an example like (28) in which
either noun phrase may be associated with the reflexive as its
antecedent.

>(28) The rich girl talked to the poor girl about herself

The interpretation of (28) is ambiguous in that either the
noun phrase the rich girl or the noun phrase the poor girl may
be associated with the reflexive as its antecedent. The possibility of such an ambiguity does not exist in those languages
in which the antecedents associated with reflexives are invariably subject noun phrases. For instance, in German the two
interpretations of (28) are expressed by two distinct sentences,
namely (29) and (30).

>(29) Die reiche Frau hat mit der armen Frau ueber sie gesprochen

>(30) Die reiche Frau hat mit der armen Frau ueber sich gesprochen

In sentence (29) it is possible to associate the noun phrase
der armen Frau in the prepositional object though not with the

noun phrase _die reiche Frau_ in the subject with the anaphoric
pronoun _sie_ as its antecedent. In sentence (30), on the other
hand, it is the subject noun phrase _die reiche Frau_ and not
the noun phrase _der armen Frau_ in the prepositional object
that is associated with the reflexive _sich_ as its antecedent.

It has already been pointed out that another property
with respect to which the syntax of reflexives resembles the
syntax of bound pronouns concerns the sentential ancestry of
reflexives and their antecedents. Just as bound anaphoric
pronouns, reflexives must be associated with antecedent noun
phrases that have the same sentential ancestry as they do.
Consider, for instance, the ill-formed sentence shown in (31).

(31) *Each candidate hopes the convention will
nominate himself

According to the usual assumptions about sentential structure,
the sentential phrase embedded in (31) can be represented informally as _The convention will nominate himself_. It is
obvious that the reflexive _himself_ is a constituent of the
embedded sentential phrase and, indirectly, of the matrix
sentence. The noun phrase _each candidate_ is a constituent of
the matrix sentence and not of the sentential phrase embedded
in it. (The noun phrase _the convention_ does not enter into the

discussion because it is not an appropriate antecedent of the reflexive himself under any conditions.) Though the noun phrase each candidate is otherwise an appropriate antecedent of the reflexive himself, example (31) is ill-formed. This is because it is not possible to associate the reflexive with an antecedent that does not have the same sentential ancestry. Much the same can be said with reference to the ill-formed sentence in example (32).

(32) *That the poor girl won pleased herself

On the usual assumptions about sentential structure, sentence (32) can be analyzed as a matrix sentence of the form That S pleased herself where in place of S the sentential phrase The poor girl won is embedded. The noun phrase the poor girl is a constituent of the embedded sentential phrase as well as a constituent of the matrix sentence. The reflexive herself is a constituent of the matrix sentence alone. Though the noun phrase the poor girl is otherwise an appropriate antecedent of the reflexive herself, in (32) this noun phrase can not be associated with the reflexive as its antecedent because a reflexive and its antecedent must have the same sentential ancestry. Since it is not possible to associate the reflexive with an appropriate antecedent, sentence (32) is ill-formed.

Both the transformational and the phrase structure theory of reflexivization allow one to relate the condition that a reflexive and its antecedent must have the same sentential ancestry to the insertion prohibition. To do this within the framework of the transformational theory, it is necessary to formulate the reflexivization procedure in such a way that it involves the introduction of new morphological material. The reflexivization procedure as it is formulated by Chomsky (1965), for instance, introduces the new morphological element _self_. This new element can not be inserted into a sentential phrase that is embedded in the phrase on which the reflexivization transformation applying cyclically is operating, because the cycle of transformational rules will already have applied to the embedded phrase. The phrase structure theory of reflexivization interprets the restriction on the sentential ancestry of reflexives and their antecedents as a restriction on the sentential ancestry of bound pronouns and their antecedents. Reflexives are represented as restricted possessives with the head noun _self_ and an unspecified determiner. Later the contents of the determiner are specified by a copying transformation. This transformation which is assumed to apply cyclically is restricted in its operation by the insertion prohibition. When applying to a particular sentential phrase, the copying transformation can not insert a copy into a sentential phrase that is embedded in the particular phrase to which it is applying. (Whenever the determiner of a restricted possessive is not specified, the structure containing it is eventually rejected.)

Both in the transformational and the phrase structure theory one can appeal to the insertion prohibition to ensure that reflexives and their antecedents have the same sentential ancestry, because in either theory the process by which reflexives are derived is subject to this constraint. In order for the insertion prohibition to apply, however, it was necessary to assume that this process is cyclical. This assumption can be motivated by the following considerations. Once a reflexive has been derived, it is necessary to prevent the relative linear order of the reflexive and its antecedent from being inverted by certain rules but not by certain others. On the one hand, the relative linear order of a reflexive and its antecedent may be inverted by the rule of verb phrase preposing. Given a structure like (33) the rule of verb phrase preposing may apply to its second conjunct, the sentential phrase she did hurt herself, to derive the sentence shown in (34).

(33) The young lady said she would hurt herself
and she did hurt herself

(34) The young lady said she would hurt herself
and hurt herself she did

Since in either theory the process by which reflexives are derived operates in a left to right fashion from the antecedent to the reflexive (or other restricted possessive), it is necessary for the antecedent of a reflexive to be to its left at the point it is derived. Therefore, the rule of verb phrase preposing which may have the effect of placing the antecedent of a reflexive to the right of the reflexive it is associated with must in either of the theories follow the rule or rules by which reflexives are derived.

On the other hand, once a reflexive has been derived, it is not possible for the relative linear order of the reflexive and its antecedent to be inverted by certain other rules without causing a violation. For instance, if after the reflexive in sentence (24) has been derived the passivization process were to apply to this sentence, then the ill-formed sentence shown in example (35) would result.

(35) *Herself was hurt by the poor girl

One can avoid this consequence by ordering the passivization process, so that it precedes the derivation of reflexives. Whenever the passivization process and the procedure by which reflexives are derived apply to the same sentential phrase and therefore on the same cycle, as they do in the derivation of sentence (35), then passivization must precede the derivation of reflexives.

The process of passivization is known to be cyclical. Since it must precede the process that derives reflexives whenever both apply on the same cycle, the process that derives reflexives must be either cyclical itself or else last cyclical or post-cyclical. To further narrow down the possibilities consider a sentence like (36).

(36) No one was expected to hurt himself

Sentence (36) consists of a matrix sentence No one expected S with the complement phrase to hurt himself embedded in place of the S. In the structure underlying this sentence the embedded complement phrase had as a subject the noun phrase no one, the derived subject of the matrix sentence. As such it was the grammatical antecedent of the reflexive in the complement noun phrase. Once this noun phrase has been extracted from the complement, it fails to meet the condition on the sentential ancestry of reflexives and their grammatical antecedents. Therefore, the reflexive must be derived prior to this. Subsequently, however, this noun phrase may undergo the passivization process as example (36) shows. It follows that in particular derivations reflexives must be derived before the passivization process applies. This rules out post-cyclical ordering as a possibility for the process by which reflexives are derived, since in these derivations reflexives are derived prior to the cyclical passivization process. Last cyclical ordering can also be ruled out, because in example (36) the reflexive is derived in an embedded sentential phrase and, therefore, it can not possibly occur on the last cycle. The only remaining possibility is that reflexives are derived by a cyclical process.

The rule of verb phrase preposing, which may follow the derivation of a reflexive, inverting the relative linear order of the reflexive and its antecedent without producing a violation, is according to the analysis of Emonds (1970) a root transformation. Indeed, it appears that all root transformations may follow the derivation of reflexives, without producing violations when they invert the relative linear order of a reflexive and its antecedent. The passivization process, on the other hand, which may also cause the relative linear order of a reflexive and its grammatical antecedent to be inverted may not follow the derivation of reflexives. The rule or rules involved in passivization are on Emonds' analysis structure preserving and it seems that all structure preserving transformations must precede the derivation of reflexives in order not to produce violations by inverting the relative linear order of a given reflexive and its antecedent. The derivation of reflexives is itself a structure preserving process. On the assumptions of the transformation theory of reflexivization the derivation of reflexives is effected by substituting a reflexive for an underlying constituent that meets certain conditions of identity with respect to the reflexive. On the other hand, the copying procedure of the phrase structure theory substitutes an appropriate form for the unspecified determiner of a restricted possessive with the head noun <u>self</u>. This substitution is also structure preserving.

To motivate the insertion prohibition, Chomsky (1965) draws on the formulation of the transformational procedure to derive reflexives mentioned above. Though the results of the present study conflict with such a formulation, this is not damaging to the insertion prohibition. In particular, the formulation of the derivation of reflexives in the way outlined in this chapter is consistent with the insertion prohibition. So are the rules given in Dougherty (1968) to derive a sentence like *The candidates attacked each other* from the structure underlying the sentence *Each candidate attacked the other* by moving each from the noun phrase *each candidate* to the noun phrase *the other*. Kayne (1969) has found that in French the insertion prohibition suitably restricts the movement of *tous* and *meme* so that no special restrictions need be put on the transformations involved. Furthermore, the restrictions on the movements of enclitics in Serbo-Croatian discussed by Browne (1967) can be interpreted from this point of view.

While positive evidence for the insertion prohibition is mounting, counter-examples to it are, for independent reasons, being reanalyzed in terms that are compatible with it. For instance, the complementizer placement transformation, which has the effect of inserting an appropriate complementizer into a sentential phrase to which the cycle of transformational rules has already applied, would constitute a serious counter-example to the insertion prohibition. Bresnan (1970) has shown, however, that complementizers must be generated in the base and that there is no need for a rule that inserts complementizers in the way described.

Returning to the discussion of the parallelism between the syntax of reflexives and the syntax of restricted possessives, one can observe that as in the case of bound pronouns, there are several conditions that limit the set of possible antecedents of reflexives. For one, the antecedents of reflexives may not be possessive determiners or single coordinate conjuncts. This requirement is illustrated by the ill-formedness of sentences (37) and (38).

>(37) *The little girl's father hurt herself
>
>(38) *The little girl and the friendly gentleman hurt herself

Though the noun phrase <u>the little girl</u> as such is an appropriate antecedent of the reflexive <u>herself</u>, as a possessive determiner or a single coordinate conjunct it can not function as the required antecedent of a reflexive.

Particular formulations of the transformation theory of reflexivization have attempted to accommodate this restriction on antecedents. Within the framework of the phrase structure theory no explanation has been attempted and none will be offered here. The fact that on theory has been developed so as to provide an explanation for this restriction and the other has not does not constitute an advantage of the one over the other. The exclusion of possessive determiners and single coordinate conjuncts from the set of possible antecedents of bound anaphoric pronouns must be accounted for irrespective of the question of reflexives. Whatever the explanation of this exclusion might be, the phrase structure theory appeals to it to explain why possessive determiners and single coordinate conjuncts are not possible antecedents of reflexives.

Furthermore, it is required that the antecedent of a reflexive be analyzable as a single constituent. Sentence (39) is ill-formed because it fails to meet this condition.

(39) *The young lady showed the gentleman themselves

Violations of this kind illustrated by sentence (39) have not been discussed within the context of the transformational theory of reflexivization. No explanation consistent with this framework has been offered and no such explanation will be supplied here. Within the phrase structure theory this kind of violation is explained by the condition requiring that the antecedent of a bound pronoun be analyzable as single constituent. On the assumptions of this theory, reflexives are represented as restricted possessives with the head noun __self__ and a determiner that is initially unspecified. A transformational copying procedure later specified the contents of these determiners by substituting bound pronouns. Like all transformations, the copying transformation that is a part of this procedure operates on constituents. Hence, it can not copy two or more nodes that are not a constituent, which fact accounts for the observed restriction.

It has been noted above that the antecedent associated with a given bound pronoun is to its left. Similarly, the antecedent associated with a given reflexive is to its left. Sentences that fail to satisfy this condition on the relative linear order of reflexives and their antecedents are ill-formed. Sentence (40), which has a reflexive as a derived subject, is a case in point.

(40) *Herself was hurt by the young lady

The fact that there is no suitable noun phrase to the left of the reflexive in sentence (40) accounts for the violation. Within the transformational theory of reflexivization this is accounted for by a condition on the relative linear order of reflexives and their antecedents. Reflexivization operates on a pair of noun phrases substituting an appropriate reflexive for one and leaving the other, the antecedent, unchanged. The formulation of this procedure is such that the unchanged antecedent noun phrase is to the left of the noun phrase for which the reflexive is substituted. This explanation for the observed relative linear order of reflexives and their antecedents is specific to reflexives and their antecedents. It is in no way related to the fact that anaphoric pronouns (in some dialects only bound anaphoric pronouns) and their antecedents are subject to the same restriction on their relative linear order whenever they both have the same sentential ancestry. The transformational theory of reflexivization would, therefore, be quite consistent with the discovery, if it were a fact, that the restriction on the relative linear order of anaphoric pronouns and their antecedents (when both are of the same sentential ancestry) is not the same as with reflexives and their antecedents. If it were found to be a fact that the antecedents of anaphoric pronouns must be to their right rather than to their left, one would not have to complicate the grammar to accommodate this fact. This is not so, however, in the case of the phrase structure theory of reflexivization. On the assumptions of this theory, the observed relative linear order of reflexives and their antecedents is related to the observed linear order of anaphoric pronouns and their antecedents. Reflexives are analyzed as restricted possessives, the determiners of which consist of bound anaphoric pronouns.

Any anaphoric pronoun that is associated with an antecedent that has the same sentential ancestry as it does must be to the left of its antecedent. While free anaphoric pronouns may have the same sentential ancestry as their antecedents, bound anaphoric pronouns must, at the point at which they are generated, have the same sentential ancestry as their antecedents. Consequently, the antecedent of a bound anaphoric pronoun must at this point be to its left. The antecedent of a reflexive must therefore also be to its left, since on the analysis of this theory it is the antecedent of the bound anaphoric pronoun in the determiner of the reflexive. Thus, the relative linear order of reflexives is necessarily the same as that of anaphoric pronouns and their antecedents, when both pronoun and antecedent have the same sentential ancestry. This explanation for the observed relative linear order of reflexives and the antecedent noun phrases they are associated with is simpler than the one provided by the transformational theory of reflexivization. It does not require the statement of a condition on the relative linear order of reflexives and their antecedents that is specific to reflexives and their antecedents. The explanation for the observed relative linear order of reflexives and their antecedents is related to the condition on the relative linear order of anaphoric pronouns and their antecedents, a condition that is required irrespective of the question of reflexivization. In relating the observed relative linear order of reflexives and their antecedents to the observed relative linear order of anaphoric pronouns and their antecedents, the phrase structure theory is also making a stronger claim than the transformational theory of reflexivization. This claim would not be compatible with the discovery, if it were a fact, that the observed linear order of reflexives and their antecedents is not the same as that of anaphoric pronouns and their antecedents (when both are of the same sentential ancestry). If it were found to be a fact that the antecedent of an anaphoric pronoun must be to its right rather than to its left, then, in order to account for this fact, the complexity of the grammar would have to be increased.

The cross-over constraint proposed by Postal (1968a) suggests a way of relating the observed relative linear order of reflexives and their antecedents to the observed relative linear order of anaphoric pronouns and their antecedents that is consistent with the transformational theory of reflexivization. The constraint in question is concerned with the relative order of pairs of noun phrases, one of which is the antecedent of the other, or, in the words of Postal (1968a), pairs of <u>co-referential nominals</u>. One could relate the order of reflexives and their antecedents to the order of anaphoric pronouns and their antecedents in terms of this constraint, because it makes no distinction between anaphoric pronouns and their antecedents, on the one hand, and reflexives and their antecedents, on the other. Hence, it is appropriate to consider the question of the relative linear order of two coreferent noun phrases from this point of view. This particular approach to this question is based on the contention that there exists a relation between certain restrictions on the surface structure distribution of coreferent noun phrases and the movement of noun phrases by transformation. "It is argued that the observed constraints on the distribution of coreferent nominals (noun phrases) are directly related to the movement of nominals by transformational rules. That is, it is claimed that the restrictions are a function of restrictions on the operation of transformational rules which move nominals." (Postal (1968a) p. 3) To express this relation between the restricted surface structure distribution of coreferent noun phrases and their movement by transformational rules, Postal advances a principle governing the operation of those transformations that move noun phrases, in particular derivations. This principle, which he calls the Cross-Over Constraint, states roughly that the operation of a movement transformation to invert the relative linear order of two coreferent noun phrases produces a violation given that certain conditions qualifying its applicability are met. Postal motivates the Cross-Over Constraint by considerations relating to sentences like (41)-(44).

(41) I talked to her about herself
(42) *I talked about herself to her
(43) *I talked to herself about her
(44) *I talked about her to herself

Two transformational processes are relevant to the discussion of (41)-(44): About Movement and reflexivization, applying in that order. About Movement converts structures like that underlying <u>Mary talked to John about herself</u> into structures like that underlying <u>Mary talked about herself to John</u>. Reflexivization substitutes an appropriate reflexive for one of a pair of noun phrases meeting certain conditions of identity given that they both have the same sentential ancestry. The substitution is made for the noun phrase on the right. The noun phrase on the left, the antecedent, remains unchanged. Sentences such as (41)-(44) are assumed to have an underlying

word order in which the to-phrase precedes the about-phrase.
The relative order of these phrases can be optionally inverted
by About Movement. Thus, (41) and (43) represent the underlying word order while (42) and (44) reflect the operation of
the About Movement transformation. Sentences (42) and (43),
however, are not generated. Reflexivization requires that
there be a suitable antecedent to the left of the noun phrase
for which the reflexive is substituted, and these sentences
do not meet this condition. In (44), however, this condition
is met, and, hence, its ill-formedness can not be related to
reflexivization.

Sentences (41) and (44) can be seen to be transformationally related by tracing them back to the structures underlying
them. Both derive from a common deep structure. In this
structure the head of the to-phrase and the head of the about-phrase meet the identity condition that characterizes the transformational theory of reflexivization. One can represent this
structure schematically as I talked to X about X, the two occurrences of X standing for coreferent noun phrases. The
derivation of (41) and (44) differs only in that (44) has
undergone About Movement while (41) has not. Postal credits
the ill-formedness of (44) to this fact. In particular, the
derivation of (44) (and the derivation of (42) as well) involves

the inversion of the relative order of two coreferent noun phrases by About Movement. This inversion operation meets the conditions on the applicability of the Cross-Over Constraint, and, hence, it is recorded as a violation. The Cross-Over Constraint relates the ill-formedness of (44), i.e., the restriction on the distribution of coreferent noun phrases in the *to*-phrase and the *about*-phrase, to the inversion of their relative order by the About Movement transformation. This makes sense only if the structure to which the movement transformation applies actually incurs a violation through the operation of this transformation. This appears to be the case here, given Postal's assumptions. Sentence (41), the derivation of which is identical to the derivation of (44) except that About Movement has not applied, does not suffer from any defect. Hence, the structure underlying (41) must be well-formed. However, the derivation of (44) from the same well-formed deep structure that underlies (41) does yield an ill-formed sentence. Hence, the specific contribution of the About Movement transformation to the derivation of (44), which differs from the derivation of (41) only in the operation of this transformation, is to make the resultant sentence ill-formed.

The claim that (41) and (44) are transformationally related depends curcially on the existence of a transformational process of reflexivization which, as it was characterized above, derives reflexives by substitution for one of a pair of noun phrases whose underlying representations meet certain conditions of identity. These are the assumptions of the transformational theory of reflexivization which will be shown directly to be inadequate. The phrase structure theory of reflexivization, on the other hand, represents reflexives in the deep structure as possessives with the head noun self. Given the phrase structure theory, (41) and (44) can not be related transformationally. The structure from which sentence (41) derives can be represented informally as (41) itself. Sentence (44) is derived by About Movement from an underlying structure that can be represented informally as (43). On this view, the ill-formed sentence (44) derives from a structure that has no well-formed surface structure whether or not About Movement applies to it. Hence, it is an open question whether or not the operation of the About Movement transformation makes a contribution to the ill-formedness of (44). But it must be shown that the operation of the About Movement transformation does make such a contribution if the Cross-Over Constraint as formulated is to be maintained, because it applies to this particular derivation. One would, for example, have to show that (44), the derivation of which differs from that of (43) only in the operation of the About Movement transformation, is more severely ill-formed than (43).

An alternate account of (41)-(44) based on the assumption that (41) and (44) are not transformationally related, would take roughly the following form. Sentences (41) and (42) have a common deep structure. Sentences (43) and (44) have a common deep structure different from that of (41) and (42). The deep structure of (41) and (42) is well-formed; the deep structure of (43) and (44) is ill-formed. It is a condition of the reflexivization process that there be a suitable antecedent to the left of any given reflexive. This condition is tested after About Movement. Sentence (42) is blocked because it fails to meet this condition. Sentences (43) and (44) are blocked because of a special condition which requires that the subject of the sentence be associated with any reflexive in the to-phrase as its antecedent. Sentences (46)-(49), in which the to-phrase is filled by a reciprocal, provide independent evidence for this condition.

(46) *I talked to each other about them

(47) *I talked about them to each other

The special condition that accounts for the ill-formedness of
the structure underlying (43) and (44) can be extended to
account for the ill-formedness of the structure underlying (46)
and (47). The subject of the sentence must be associated with
any possible reciprocal in the to-phrase as its antecedent.
The fact that sentences (48) and (49) are well-formed is, of
course, consistent with this requirement.

    (48)   They talked to each other about me

    (49)   They talked about me to each other

On the assumption that (41) and (44) are not transformationally
related, the Cross-Over Constraint is not needed to account
for (41)-(44). An alternate account for these sentences based
on this assumption, however, requires a special condition to
rule out the ill-formed structure that underlies (43) and (44)
and also (46) and (47). If the Cross-Over Constraint were disconfirmed completely, this might be taken as an argument against
such an alternative.

Therefore, consider certain unhappy consequences of the
Cross-Over Constraint. Sentences (50) and (51), where (51) is
derived from the structure underlying (50) by About Movement,
are a case in point.

    (50)   I talked to myself about myself

(51) I talked about myself to myself

The derivation of (51) involves the inversion of the relative order of two coreferent noun phrases. In the absence of conditions qualifying the applicability of the Cross-Over Constraint, it would predict that, because of this, (51) is ill-formed. This situation does not arise, however. The Cross-Over Constraint is applicable only if at the point where the inversion occurs, neither of the two noun phrases whose relative order is inverted has undergone reflexivization or pronominalization. In Postal's terminology, both coreferents must be Pronominal Virgins as a precondition on the applicability of the Cross-Over Constraint. Given the deep structure Postal assigns the kind of sentence under discussion, this condition allows About Movement to apply in the derivation of (51) without causing a violation of the Cross-Over Constraint. In particular, sentences (50) and (51) are assigned the deep structure schematically represented as (52), which, as Postal concedes, has no independent justification.

(52) $[_{S_3} [_{S_1}$ I talked to me $_{S_1}] [_{S_2}$ X was about me $_{S_2}] _{S_3}]$

On the cycle defined by S_1 reflexivization substitutes a reflexive for the head of the to-phrase. Subsequently, the about-phrase and the rest of the structure are inserted into the same

sentence by a transformation rule which Postal calls About
Insertion. About Movement then applies to invert the relative
order of the coreferent noun phrases in the head of the to-
phrase and the about-phrase. This is not recorded as a violation because the head of the to-phrase has, at this point,
already undergone reflexivization. Since it is not the case
that both coreferent noun phrases are Pronominal Virgins at
the point at which the About Movement transformation operates,
the inversion operation is not subject to the Cross-Over
Constraint. Finally, reflexivization applies again to substitute an appropriate reflexive for the head of the about-
phrase.

In the alternate account of these facts based on the
phrase structure theory of reflexivization, both (50) and (51)
meet the condition that a reflexive must have a suitable antecedent to its left. Furthermore, both sentences meet the
special condition required to account for the ill-formedness
of the structure underlying (43) and (44): The reflexive in
the to-phrase is associated with the subject. By contrast with
the cumbersome and ad hoc analysis of (50) and (51) required by
the Cross-Over Constraint, the elegance of the alternate account
strongly suggests that the Cross-Over Constraint is in error.

The argument advanced so far, however, is not conclusive.
Consider, therefore, an example of the following sort. Given
a string ABC in which B and C are coreferent noun phrases.
Furthermore, given two transformations: The first inverts the
last two elements of any string. The second, applying in
order after the first, takes the last element of a string and
moves it to the initial position. Allowing these transformations
to apply in order to ABC, one obtains the following derivation.

    (53) ABC   underlying string

    (54) ACB   first transformation

    (55) BAC   second transformation

Assuming that the Cross-Over Constraint applies to the operation
of both transformations in the above derivation, both (54) and
(55) would be predicted to be ill-formed. In fact, given the
assumption that compounded violations yield more deviant
structures, an assumption which Postal accepts, (55) should be
severely ill-formed. While the derivation of (54) involves a
single violation of the Cross-Over Constraint, the derivation
of (55) involves two. Examples of this sort exist in natural
languages. For instance, Jackendoff (1969) (ch. 2, (253)) has
pointed out that the derivation of (58) given schematically in
(56)-(58) involves two violations of this constraint.

(56) You talked to whom about himself   underlying word order

(57) You talked about himself to whom   About Movement

(58) Whom did you talk about himself to   WH fronting

The Cross-Over Constraint is violated by the operation of About Movement on the structure represented by (56) and by the operation of WH fronting, Postal's WH Q-Movement, on the structure represented by (57). Consequently, (58) is predicted to be severely ill-formed. This prediction, however, is false.

The alternate account based on the phrase structure theory of reflexivization makes the right prediction. In (58), though not in (57), the condition that a reflexive must have a suitable antecedent to its left is met. On the basis of the false prediction it makes in this instance, the Cross-Over Constraint must be rejected.

Even if there were no difficulties with the Cross-Over Constraint, it would not be possible to relate the observed relative linear order of reflexives and their antecedents to the relative linear order of anaphoric pronouns and their antecedents in terms of the constraint. The reason for this is the fact that the possessive determiners which figure prominently among the examples of pronouns that are associated with antecedents which have the same sentential ancestry as they (the same conditions under which reflexives are associated with their antecedents) are exempt from it.

Though the examples used in the exposition of the properties of reflexives and the conditions that they and their antecedents must satisfy all involve sentential phrases with verbal heads and sentential phrases with verbal heads embedded in sentential phrases with verbal heads, the same observations can be made in relation to sentential phrases with nominal heads. Since sentential phrases with nominal heads must always be embedded, however, these examples appear to be more complicated, and it is for this reason that they were not used. Nevertheless, all that was said above with regard to the conditions that reflexives and their antecedents (and generally the bound anaphoric pronouns and their antecedents) must meet holds here as well. First, well-formedness requires that it be possible to associate a reflexive with an appropriate antecedent. Sentence (59) meets this condition and is well-formed.

    (59) The rich girl saw the young man's picture of himself

In example (59) the reflexive is a constituent of the sentential phrase The young man's picture of himself, the head of which is the noun picture. The noun phrase the young man's in the specifier of this phrase is associated with the reflexive as its antecedent. Thus, the reflexive and its antecedent have the same sentential ancestry. Consider, however, sentence (60).

(60) *The rich girl saw the young men's picture of himself

The structure underlying sentence (60) is the same as that underlying sentence (59) except that the specifier of the embedded sentential phrase is in the plural rather than in the singular. Because of this it is not possible to associate the specifier of the embedded phrase with the reflexive as its antecedent. As a consequence, the sentence is ill-formed.

Second, a reflexive and its grammatical antecedent must, at the point at which the reflexive is derived, have the same sentential ancestry. Consider the ill-formed example given in (61) in the light of this requirement.

(61) *The rich girl saw the young man's picture of herself

The reflexive herself in example (61) is a constituent of the embedded sentential phrase the young man's picture of herself which has the noun picture as a head. This phrase is embedded in the matrix The rich girl saw NP in place of the NP. At no stage in the derivation of sentence (61) can the reflexive in the embedded sentential phrase be associated with an appropriate antecedent that has the same sentential ancestry as it does. As a consequence, sentence (61) is ill-formed.

Thirdly, possessive determiners and single coordinate conjuncts are not valid antecedents of reflexives. First consider example (59) in the light of the claim that possessive determiners are not valid antecedents of reflexives. In this example, the specifier of the embedded sentential phrase <u>the young man's picture of himself</u> is associated with the reflexive as its antecedent. The specifier of this phrase is morphologically indistinguishable from the possessive determiner of the noun phrase <u>the young man's mother</u>. As a result the fact that it is the grammatical antecedent of the reflexive in sentence (59) might be interpreted as conflicting with this requirement. The two phrases are not comparable, however. The phrase <u>the young man's picture of himself</u> has the internal structure of a sentence. In particular, it has a complement. The phrase <u>the young man's mother</u>, on the other hand, has the internal structure of a noun and it does not allow complements. Thus, the specifier of the sentential phrase embedded in sentence (59) is differentiated from the possessive determiner of the noun phrase the young man's mother in terms of the possible expansions of these phrases. To illustrate the validity of the claim that reflexives can not be associated with antecedent noun phrases that are possessive determiners on the basis of a sentence in which the reflexive is a constituent of a sentential phrase with a nominal head, one must construct an example like (62).

(62) *The rich girl saw the young man's mother's picture of himself

The sentential phrase the young man's mother's picture of himself which is embedded in sentence (62) has a nominal head. The specifier of this phrase is the noun phrase the young man's mother which has a possessive determiner consisting of the noun phrase the young man. Though the noun phrase the young man is in all other respects an appropriate antecedent for the reflexive himself, in this case it can not be associated with the reflexive as its antecedent because it is a possessive determiner.

The claim that reflexives can not be associated with antecedent noun phrases consisting of single coordinate conjuncts can also be illustrated with an example of this kind. Consider, for example, sentence (63).

(63) *The young girl saw the young man's and his
mother's picture of himself

The sentential phrase containing the reflexive is <u>the young man's and his mother's picture of himself</u>. The reflexive in this phrase can not be associated with the noun phrase <u>the young man's</u> that is one of the coordinate conjuncts making up the specifier of this phrase though this noun phrase would otherwise be an appropriate antecedent for the reflexive. The reason for this is that the noun phrase in question is a single coordinate conjunct.

One could similarly construct examples to illustrate the discussion of the relative linear order of reflexives and their antecedents using reflexives that are constituents of sentential phrases with nominal heads, but since this would not add to the discussion, this will not be done. Instead, the discussion turns to the crucial example that discriminates between the transformational and the phrase structure theories of reflexivization.

To put the following into perspective, a certain device to account for the dependency between bound anaphoric pronouns and their antecedents was motivated. It had the form of a copying procedure. Quite apart from the question of reflexivi-

the noun picture. The noun phrase the young man's in the specifier of this phrase is associated with the reflexive as its antecedent. Thus, the reflexive and its antecedent have the same sentential ancestry. Consider, however, sentence (60).

(60) *The rich girl saw the young men's picture of himself

The structure underlying sentence (60) is the same as that underlying sentence (59) except that the specifier of the embedded sentential phrase is in the plural rather than in the singular. Because of this it is not possible to associate the specifier of the embedded phrase with the reflexive as its antecedent. As a consequence, the sentence is ill-formed.

Second, a reflexive and its grammatical antecedent must, at the point at which the reflexive is derived, have the same sentential ancestry. Consider the ill-formed example given in (61) in the light of this requirement.

(61) *The rich girl saw the young man's picture of herself

The reflexive herself in example (61) is a constituent of the embedded sentential phrase the young man's picture of herself which has the noun picture as a head. This phrase is embedded in the matrix The rich girl saw NP in place of the NP. At no stage in the derivation of sentence (61) can the reflexive in the embedded sentential phrase be associated with an appropriate antecedent that has the same sentential ancestry as it does. As a consequence, sentence (61) is ill-formed.

Thirdly, possessive determiners and single coordinate conjuncts are not valid antecedents of reflexives. First consider example (59) in the light of the claim that possessive determiners are not valid antecedents of reflexives. In this example, the specifier of the embedded sentential phrase <u>the young man's picture of himself</u> is associated with the reflexive as its antecedent. The specifier of this phrase is morphologically indistinguishable from the possessive determiner of the noun phrase <u>the young man's mother</u>. As a result the fact that it is the grammatical antecedent of the reflexive in sentence (59) might be interpreted as conflicting with this requirement. The two phrases are not comparable, however. The phrase <u>the young man's picture of himself</u> has the internal structure of a sentence. In particular, it has a complement. The phrase <u>the young man's mother</u>, on the other hand, has the internal structure of a noun and it does not allow complements. Thus, the specifier of the sentential phrase embedded in sentence (59) is differentiated from the possessive determiner of the

zation, the existence of bound pronouns by itself requires that this or some equivalent device be a part of the grammar of English. It was shown that this device could be used to account for the observed dependency between reflexives and their antecedents on the assumption that reflexives are restricted possessives with the head noun <u>self</u> and with bound pronouns as determiners. (This is the basic assumption of the phrase structure theory of reflexivization.) Since some form of this device must be part of any grammar of English, a grammar that incorporates the transformational theory of reflexivization can account for reflexives in two ways: firstly, in terms of the transformational theory and, secondly, in terms of the phrase structure theory of reflexivization. This might lead one to think that such a grammar is excessively powerful. This issue does not arise, however, since these two theories of reflexivization make conflicting claims about the syntactic distribution of reflexives. Hence, one need only determine what the conflicting predictions of these theories are, and the facts of English will determine which, if either, makes the right prediction. The conflict involves the identity condition imposed by the transformational theory of reflexivization. In the transformational theory, a reflexive has an underlying representation that has the same syntactic properties as its antecedent. The transformational theory of reflexivization, therefore, claims that a reflexive can not occur in an environment in which a noun phrase with the syntactic properties of its antecedent can not occur. Specifically, it predicts that "there are sentences of the form $\underline{NP_1 + Verb + Reflexive\ Pronoun + Y}$ just in case one can also find sentences of the form $\underline{NP_2 + Verb + NP_1 + Y}$. That is, those verbs which take reflexive pronoun 'objects' are just those which can elsewhere occur with 'objects' identical to the 'subjects' of the reflexive sentences." (Postal (1964b), p.250) The phrase structure theory, on the other hand, claims that in general reflexives can occur wherever a noun phrase, the head of which has the same syntactic properties as the noun self, can occur. On the assumptions of the phrase structure theory of reflexivization, reflexives invariably have the same syntactic properties irrespective of their particular antecedent. Specifically, it is possible that a reflexive have an antecedent with syntactic properties different from those of self. Hence, a crucial example for the phrase structure theory would be one in which a reflexive can occur, though the noun phrase underlying its antecedent can not. The phrase structure theory predicts that this may be possible; the transformational theory claims that this is not possible.

Just such an example was discussed by Lees and Klima (1963). Their example involves the verb <u>express</u> in a sentence like (64). Other sentences illustrating the same point are given in (65) and (66).

    (64)   The poor girl expressed herself

    (65)   A good teacher repeats himself

    (66)   Every young man needs to prove himself

On the assumptions of the transformational theory of reflexivization the noun phrase <u>the poor girl</u> would have to be a possible object complement of <u>express</u>, since this is the underlying representation for the reflexive object in (64). This, however, is not generally so as one can see in (67).

    (67) *The friendly gentleman expressed the poor girl

The evidence of (64) and (67) selects the phrase structure theory over the transformational theory of reflexivization. In the phrase structure theory a reflexive may occupy a position which its antecedent may not occupy.

Enlarging on this a bit, the transformational theory of reflexivization assumes that the underlying representation of a reflexive has the same syntactic properties as its antecedent.

Therefore, the existence of a reflexive sentence like (64) prevents one from categorically excluding the poor girl and all noun phrases with the same syntactic properties from the object complement of express. Not all sentences where express has an object complement with these properties are well-formed, however, as one can see in (67). In fact, object complements of this particular kind are allowed only when they are subsequently reflexivized. The transformational theory of reflexivization, if it is to be maintained in spite of the evidence against it, must impose a condition to this effect on the set of verbs of which express is an instance. The phrase structure theory of reflexivization can handle these cases directly by attributing different syntactic properties to self, on the one hand, and the poor girl, on the other, and by imposing a selectional restriction on the object complement of express which allows the former while it excludes the latter. Even though this solution appears to be much simpler than that of the transformational theory it might still be considered ad hoc, if there were no independent evidence for exactly such a selectional restriction. This evidence comes from nominalizations of the stem express such as those in (68) and (69).

(68) the expression of self (in 17th century literature)

(69) *the expression of the poor girl

To account for the well-formedness of (68) and the ill-formedness of (69), it is necessary to exclude noun phrases with the syntactic properties of the poor girl from the complement of express while allowing noun phrases like self. This is, obviously, the same selectional restriction required to account for sentences (64) and (67). Since the evidence of these nominalizations of express is not related to reflexivization, it is clear that the selectional restriction it supports must be stated in any grammar whether it incorporates the phrase structure or the transformational theory of reflexivization. The phrase structure theory accounts for sentences (64) and (67) on the basis of this restriction. The transformational theory, on the other hand, even with the elaboration that makes it compatible with the evidence contained in sentences (64) and (67) fails to relate the nominalizations in (68) and (69) to these sentences. Hence, it fails to express the generalization that the selectional restrictions of the lexical stem express are the same whether it is realized as a verb or as a noun.

Before leaving this discussion, it is necessary to consider

certain facts that might be interpreted as counter-examples to the phrase structure theory of reflexivization. Basically, the phrase structure theory claims that reflexives are restricted possessives. Hence, any property that distinguishes reflexives from the set of restricted possessives or, indeed, from the set of possessives as a whole would have to be considered a counter-example to this theory.

Consider, for instance, that the determiners of *himself*, *itself*, and *themselves* are not in the form that possessive determiners ordinarily take. This sets these reflexives apart from ordinary possessives. In order to relate these reflexives to ordinary possessives, the phrase structure theory of reflexivization must postulate some ad hoc device that has the effect of adjusting *his* to *him*, *its* to *it*, and *their* to *them* under the appropriate conditions. (The conversion of *its-self* to *it-self* may in fact be accounted for by phonological rules. For the sake of generality, however, the conversion process would be formulated so as to substitute for each third person possessive determiner the corresponding object form of the personal pronouns, substituting *it* for *its* and vacuously *her* for *her*.) The need for such an ad hoc device is not a liability of the phrase structure theory because of the following conditions. With attributive adjectives interposed in their normal position between determiner and head, these possessives take the standard form of the possessive determiner, and no adjustment is needed: <u>his own self</u>, <u>its own self</u>, and <u>their own selves</u>. What is more, there are dialects in which there is no idiosyncracy regarding the shape of the determiners of these reflexives. In these dialects reflexives take the standard form of the possessive determiners throughout the paradigm. In view of this, if one were to start out with these reflexives represented as <u>himself</u>, <u>itself</u>, and <u>themselves</u>, then one would need an ad hoc device complementary to the one required by the phrase structure theory to change these reflexives to standard possessive form whenever they have attributive adjectives modifying them or in those dialects in which the paradigm has been regularized everywhere. Furthermore, on this analysis, the <u>possessive</u> forms are irregular, which is, of course, not in accord with the fact that all other reflexives are bona fide possessives. Therefore, while this idiosyncracy of the determiners of certain reflexives does indeed distinguish reflexives when they are analyzed as possessives from all other possessives, it does not put the phrase structure theory of reflexivization at a disadvantage with respect to any other reflexivization theory. Hence, it can not be counted against the phrase structure theory.

Another property of reflexives that might be interpreted as distinguishing them from restricted possessives or, indeed, possessives in general is the fact that a reflexive and its determiner usually have the same grammatical number: myself not myselves, ourselves not ourself. As one can see from an example such as the restricted possessive in I blinked my eyes (=4), this property of reflexives is not a property of the set of restricted possessives as such. Nor, for that matter, is it a property of possessives in general. A certain subset of restricted possessives, however, of which those in The poor girl lost her mind (=1) and We nodded our heads (=2) are examples, is characterized by the fact that their determiners agree with them in grammatical number. In these restricted possessives and in others like them, a discrepancy between the number of the possessive and the number of its determiner amounts to a violation as one can see in (70) and (71).

(70) *The poor girl lost her minds

(71) *We nodded our head

It is not clear whether the ill-formedness of (70) or (71)
is of a syntactic or semantic nature. But whatever it is
that accounts for the agreement in the grammatical number of
reflexives and their determiners, the fact of the agreement
is not an idiosyncracy of reflexives. Rather it is a property
of a certain subset of restricted possessives of which reflexives are only an instance. Hence, the observation that
reflexives exhibit number agreement between their determiners
and their heads can not be interpreted as a counter-example
to the phrase structure theory of reflexivization.

CHAPTER THREE

In the preceding chapter it was shown that reflexives and their antecedents must satisfy certain conditions that specifically characterize the relation between them. In particular, considerations of well-formedness require that reflexives be associated with appropriate antecedents, the lack of which is recorded as a violation. Further, reflexives and their antecedents must have the same sentential ancestry. Possessive determiners and single coordinate conjuncts can not be associated with reflexives as their antecedents. Valid antecedents are analyzable as single constituents. Finally, appropriate antecedents are to the left of the reflexives with which they are associated. This chapter is concerned with certain examples that might seem to case doubt on the validity of some of these conditions.

There are, for instance, examples involving imperatives which appear to contradict the claim that well-formedness requires that each reflexive be associated with an appropriate antecedent. While imperative sentences take reflexive objects in their surface form, there may not be antecedents associated with these reflexives. For instance, an imperative sentence such as Wash yourself (yourselves) does not contain an antecedent for the reflexive. In the case of imperatives, the absence of a suitable antecedent may not seem problematical because the transformational derivation of imperatives from underlying structures containing appropriate antecedents in the form of second person subjects is relatively uncontroversial. It has not been generally recognized, however, that other apparent counter-examples to some of the conditions that reflexives and their antecedents must satisfy are amenable to a resolution of the same kind. It may, therefore, be useful to discuss this familiar example in some detail. It will then be shown that in a variety of instances apparent counter-examples to the conditions on reflexives and their antecedents can be made to conform to these conditions if one postulates appropriate antecedents in the structures underlying the sentences in question. To postulate such antecedents simply to make certain recalcitrant examples conform to conditions to which they would otherwise constitute exceptions would, of course, be ad hoc. In each instance where an underlying antecedent is postulated, however, it can be shown to be independently motivated.

In the particular instance of imperatives, the underlying second person subject is motivated by at least the following three considerations. One: it serves to explain why, in imperatives, the only possible restricted possessive objects are those that have second person determiners such as: <u>Keep your hopes up</u>. As outlined in Chapter Two the determiner of a restricted possessive which is initially not specified is derived from its antecedent by a transformational copying procedure. In an imperative, the only source for such a determiner is the postulated second person subject. Hence, the only restricted possessive that can occupy the object position is one whose determiner derives from a second person antecedent. Two: the postulated underlying second person subject also serves to explain why tag questions appended to imperatives have second person subjects and why other subjects are excluded. The reason is that there is a dependency between the subject of a tag question and the subject of the sentence to which it is appended. This requires that the subject of the tag be a pronoun that agrees with the subject of the tagged sentence in person, number, and gender. Hence, in the case of imperatives, whose subjects are postulated to be second person, the subject of the tag must always be second person. Three: if one did not postulate an underlying subject for imperatives which manifests itself indirectly through reflexive objects and tag questions (and sometimes directly), then one would have to elaborate the rules of the base. This elaboration would be required to generate the usually subjectless surface structure of imperatives. This is undesirable since there is little independent motivation for such a structure (but see Quang (1967). On the other hand, by postulating an underlying subject for imperatives, one can reduce them to base forms of the usual subject-verb-complement form.

These three points show that independently of any considerations relating to reflexives a subject and specifically a second person subject must be postulated for the structures underlying imperatives. The existence of the underlying structures arrived at on the basis of these theoretical considerations is confirmed by the observation that these same structures underlie well-formed (imperative) sentences in which the postulated underlying constituent is still present, as, for instance, in the command You wash yourself (yourselves). To relate the postulated underlying structures with second person subjects to the usual subjectless surface forms of imperatives, it is necessary to postulate a transformational deletion rule that has the effect of deleting the subject of the structure underlying imperatives. This rule can be motivated independently by considerations relating to certain sentences that do not involve imperatives. In fact, these considerations motivate a rule that under certain conditions deletes first as well as second person subject pronouns though not third person pronouns which will be shown below. (All of the conditions that limit the operation of this rule will not be explored here.) Consider sentences like (1) and (2).

(1) It is best to keep my mind open

(2) It is best to keep your mind open

Considerations relating to the simplicity of the base rules motivate the postulation of an underlying subject for the sentential phrases embedded in (1) and (2) respectively. The first and second person pronominal determiners of the restricted possessives in the object of these embedded sentential phrases motivate the postulation of appropriate antecedents from which to derive them. Putting these two considerations together, one can motivate the postulation of appropriate antecedents associated with the determiners of the restricted possessives in the form of subject noun phrases. The existence of the postulated underlying structures arrived at on the basis of these considerations is confirmed by the existence of sentences in which these structures are mapped onto surface structures with the postulated underlying subject noun phrases intact. These sentences are shown in (3) and (4) respectively.

(3) It is best that I keep my mind open

(4) It is best that you keep your mind open

By postulating a rule that deletes first and second person subject under certain conditions that will remain to be determined exactly, one can relate the structures underlying sentences (1) and (2) to the structures underlying the respective synonymous sentences (3) and (4). It was said earlier that this rule can not delete third person subject pronouns or nouns. Consider, for example, a sentence that corresponds in structure to the sentences on which this deletion rule is known to operate but which has a third person pronoun or a noun in place of the first or second person pronoun. Such a sentence, (5) for example, does not have a well-formed variant in which the third person pronoun or noun subject has been deleted. One can see this from the ill-formedness of (6).

(5) It is best that he keep his mind open

(6) *It is best to keep his mind open

Some have sought to generalize the deletion operation illustrated by these examples with the possibility of deleting certain third person pronouns if they can be associated with appropriate antecedents. This question will be taken up at the end of this chapter, where it will be shown that this latter approach fails.

In the derivation of sentences (1) and (2) the deletion rule is operating on embedded sentential phrases. In imperative sentences, on the other hand, it is operating on sentential phrases that are not embedded. In the examples where it is operating on embedded sentential phrases, it can delete both first and second person subjects; and one would, therefore, expect that in the examples where it is operating on sentential phrases that are not embedded, it could also delete both first and second person subjects. While the imperative examples involve only the deletion of second person subjects, there are indeed comparable examples which might be interpreted as involving the deletion of first person subjects, though these examples do not constitute a productive class. Among the examples of this kind there are sentences like (7), (9), and (11), all of which have versions in which the subject has been deleted, namely, (8), (10), and (12).

(7) I am sorry to say

(8) Sorry to say

(9) I wish you were here

(10) Wish you were here

(11) I thank you

(12) Thank you

On the basis of the three points discussed earlier, one can postulate underlying second person subjects for imperative sentences. Since in any given sentence the subject is the only possible antecedent for a reflexive in object position, the fact that in imperative sentences the subject is in the second person accounts for the fact that the only possible reflexive objects are those that go with a second person antecedent. The deletion rule just motivated allows one to delete the second person subject that is present in the structures underlying imperative sentences. If one states the conditions which reflexives and their antecedents must satisfy in such a way that they only need to be satisfied prior to the deletion of imperative subjects, then imperatives with reflexive objects can no longer be interpreted as counter-examples to the condition which stipulates that in well-formed sentences it must be possible to associate each reflexive with an appropriate antecedent. Though in the absence of a subject an appropriate antecedent can not be associated with a reflexive object in the surface structure at the level at which this condition is enforced.

Imperatives of the kind illustrated above are not the only examples involving reflexives which do not appear to be associated with appropriate antecedents. For instance, sentences like (13) and (14) contain reflexives which apparently can not be associated with appropriate antecedents.

    (13)   The whole family, myself included, will go to the beach

    (14)   The whole family, yourself included, will go to the beach

Other than the fact that the reflexives in these sentences appear to constitute counter-examples to the condition that requires reflexives to be associated with appropriate antecedents, it is remarkable that they have noun phrase stress. Indeed, the well-formedness of these sentences depends on this. This is exceptional in that a reflexive as a rule has pronominal stress. One can account for both of these exceptional properties of the reflexives in sentences like (13) and (14) by deriving them from emphatic reflexives. Emphatic reflexives are quite regular with regard to the condition requiring reflexives to be associated with appropriate antecedents. Usually they immediately follow their grammatical antecedents

within the same noun phrase though they can be detached from
the antecedent and placed at the end of the sentence. Furthermore, emphatic reflexives are characterized by the fact that
they have noun phrase stress. Therefore, if the reflexives
in (13) and (14) are derived from underlying emphatic reflexives by deleting their grammatical antecedents (by a rule
similar, if not identical, to the rule just discussed), then
there is a stage in their derivation at which they can be
associated with appropriate antecedents, and, in addition, they
are necessarily given noun phrase stress. This would mean that
(13) and (14) derive from structures represented informally
as (15) and (16) respectively.

(15) The whole family, I myself included, will go
to the beach

(16) The whole family, you yourself included, will
go to the beach

The existence of the structures postulated as the source for
(13) and (14) is confirmed by the fact that they underlie well-formed surface structures with the grammatical antecedent of
the emphatic reflexive intact. To derive the structures underlying (13) and (14) from the structures underlying (15) and
(16), respectively, the grammatical antecedents of the emphatic

reflexives must be deleted. This deletion is limited to first
and second subject person pronouns, just as the cases discussed
earlier. This is shown by the fact that, while there are
sentences which are like (15) and (16) (except that in place
of the first or second person pronoun they have third person
pronouns), these sentences do not have versions in which the
antecedent of the emphatic reflexive has been deleted. This
is shown by the following two examples.

(17) The whole family, he himself included, will
go to the beach

(18) *The whole family, himself included, will go
to the beach

Though it has not received wide recognition, it has not
gone entirely unnoticed that certain reflexives which are
apparent exceptions to some of the conditions that reflexives
and their antecedents must ordinarily satisfy receive noun
phrase stress. In fact, as early as 1965, Barbara Hall Partee,
in her dissertation (Hall, (1965)), has shown that certain of
these apparently exceptional reflexives could be introduced
into the underlying structure in the form of emphatic reflexives though she has wrongly claimed that these reflexives
are contrastively stressed. Because of the possibilities

which this method of deriving reflexives opens up, it is important to consider briefly some of the conditions which restrict it. For instance, it would appear undesirable, if it were possible, to derive a sentence like I know myself from an underlying structure like I know me myself. One way of blocking such a derivation would be to limit the applicability of the rule which deletes the antecedents of emphatic reflexives; and, indeed, it appears that such a deletion is possible only in parenthetical expressions such as the ones illustrated in (13) and (14) and similar cases. But whether or nor this rule is limited in this way, the derivation under consideration is not possible, because a sentence whose subject and object agree in person is ill-formed if, as in the example at hand, they are either first or second person. Other limitations on the possibility of deriving certain reflexives from underlying emphatic reflexives will be discussed in connection with another deletion rule which allows similar derivations.

There are well-formed sentences containing reflexives that do not appear to be associated with antecedent noun phrases that have the same sentential ancestry as they do. Nevertheless, the reflexives in question are associated with antecedents. These reflexives and the antecedents with which they are associated, however, do not satisfy the conditions on reflexives and their grammatical antecedents that were established in Chapter Two. In particular, they fail to meet the condition on the sentential ancestry of reflexives and their grammatical antecedents. Published discussions of the issues raised by apparent exceptions to this condition are, for the most part, based on examples of so-called picture noun reflexives.

These are reflexives that are object complements of sentential phrases having nominal heads drawn from the set of so-called picture nouns. These discussions generally do not touch upon the important question of how the reflexives in question are stressed. Furthermore, the evidence that bears on the question of the sentential ancestry of reflexives and their antecedents is not limited to examples with reflexives contained in sentential phrases with so-called picture nouns as heads. The full range of relevant evidence also includes reflexives contained in sentential phrases with verbal heads. Take, for instance, a sentence like (19) with noun phrase stress on the reflexive. (In this and in the following examples all reflexives that have noun phrase stress are underlined.)

    (19) Each candidate hopes the convention will nominate himself[1]

The structure underlying the sentential phrase embedded in (19) can, on the usual assumptions about sentential structure, be represented informally as The convention will nominate himself. On this analysis, the reflexive contained in the embedded sentential phrase does not appear to be associated with an antecedent which has the same sentential ancestry. In particular, the noun phrase the convention, which is the only noun phrase that has the same sentential ancestry as the reflexive, is not an appropriate antecedent. As an independent sentence, this phrase would be ill-formed. If, however, as in (19), it is suitably embedded, no violation is observed. The well-formedness of (19) and other sentences like it depends in part on the possibility of associating the reflexive in the embedded sentential phrase with some appropriate noun phrase elsewhere in the sentence. Replacing this noun phrase by an otherwise suitable noun phrase which can not be associated with the reflexive as its antecedent leads to a violation. For instance, sentence (20), which is identical to (19) except that in (20) the noun phrase that in (19) is associated with the reflexive has been put into the plural, is ill-formed.

(20) *The candidates hope the convention will nominate himself

Sentence (20) is ill-formed because the reflexive in it can not be associated with an appropriate antecedent noun phrase. The conditions which determine the appropriateness of an antecedent noun phrase associated with a reflexive of this kind differ from the conditions which determine the appropriateness of an antecedent noun phrase associated with a reflexive of the kind discussed in Chapter Two. Evidently, there are two kinds of reflexivization which are distinguished by the conditions that reflexives and their antecedents must satisfy. In particular, reflexives of one kind are associated with grammatical antecedents that have the same sentential ancestry as they have. Reflexives of the other kind are associated with antecedent noun phrases that do not have the same sentential ancestry as they.

Reflexives of the kind that are associated with antecedent noun phrases that do not have the same sentential ancestry as they can be found in embedded sentential phrases with verbal heads as in the example of sentence (19), but they can also be found in embedded sentential phrases with nominal heads, as in the example of sentence (21).

(21) Each defendent challenged the prosecution's indictment of himself

Given the assumptions about sentential structure set forth in Chapter One, the structure underlying the sentential phrase containing the reflexive in (21) can be represented informally as the prosecution's indictment of himself. On this analysis, the reflexive does not appear to be associated with an antecedent noun phrase that has the same sentential ancestry as it does. Nevertheless, sentence (21), as whole, is well-formed. Its well-formedness depends on the possibility of associating the reflexive with some appropriate antecedent noun phrase elsewhere in the sentence. In this particular instance, the noun phrase in question is the noun phrase each defendent in the subject of the matrix sentence. Replacing this noun phrase by an otherwise suitable noun phrase that can not be associated with the reflexive as its antecedent results in an ill-formed structure. For instance, if the noun phrase each defendent is put into the plural, then one obtains the ill-formed structure shown in (22).

(22) *The defendents challenged the prosecution's indictment of himself

Sentence (22) is ill-formed for the same reason that sentence (20) is: In neither sentence can the reflexive be associated with an appropriate antecedent noun phrase.

Jackendoff (1969), in his discussion of reflexives that appear to be associated with antecedent noun phrases that do not have the same sentential ancestry as they do, only takes into consideration reflexives contained in sentential phrases with nominal heads. Furthermore, he limits the discussion to such sentential phrases with nominal heads that do not have lexical specifiers. A typical example of this kind would be a sentence like (23) (Jackendoff's (13)).

(23) Tom made the claim that the picture of <u>himself</u> hanging in the post office is a fraud

The well-formedness of this example does not depend on the fact that the reflexive has noun phrase stress as indicated, a fact that will be discussed directly. In (23) the sentential phrase containing the reflexive, <u>the picture of himself</u>, is the subject of the embedded sentential phrase <u>the picture of himself . . . is a fraud</u>, which phrase is embedded in place of the S in the matrix sentence <u>Tom made the claim that S</u>. The reflexive in (23) can not be associated with an antecedent noun phrase that has the same sentential ancestry as it does. The sentential phrase containing the reflexive does not provide an appropriate antecedent noun phrase. Nor does the larger phrase of which the phrase containing the reflexive is the subject.

Nevertheless, it is possible to associate the reflexive with
an antecedent noun phrase that does not have the same sentential ancestry as it does. The noun phrase in question is
the noun phrase Tom in the subject of the matrix sentence.
The well-formedness of sentence (23) as a whole depends on
the possibility of doing this. Replacing this antecedent by an
otherwise suitable noun phrase which can not be associated
with the reflexive as an antecedent would cause a violation.
One can see this in example (24) which differs from (23) only
in that it has the noun phrase Mary where (23) has the noun
phrase Tom.

(24) *Mary made the claim that the picture of

himself hanging in the post office is a fraud

Example (24), like examples (20) and (22), is ill-formed
because the reflexive can not be associated with an appropriate
antecedent.

Though example (23) is more complex than example (21),
in this connection the principal difference between them
resides in the fact that the specifier of the embedded sentential phrase containing the reflexive is a lexical formative
in one but not in the other. The principle difference between
examples (21) and (23), on the one hand, and example (19), on

the other, is that the sentential phrase containing the reflexive has a nominal head in the case of (21) and (23) while in the case of (19) it has a verbal head. With regard to the sentential ancestry of reflexives and their antecedents, examples (19), (21), and (23) all make the same point.

There are other properties that set apart those reflexives that are associated with grammatical antecedents having the same sentential ancestry as they from those that are associated with antecedents that do not have the same sentential ancestry as they. In Chapter Two it was established that whenever a reflexive and its antecedent have the same sentential ancestry then the antecedent must be analyzable as a single constituent. When a reflexive and the antecedent noun phrase with which it is associated do not have the same sentential ancestry, however, then the antecedent noun phrase need not be analyzable as a single constituent. One can see this in sentences like (25)-(27).

(25) The incumbent told his running mate that the convention had nominated themselves

(26) The rich girl showed her husband the gallery's picture of themselves

(27) The rich girl showed her husband a picture of themselves

In example (25) the two noun phrases <u>the incumbent</u> and <u>his running mate</u> can not be analyzed as a single constituent. Nevertheless, the possibility of associating the reflexive with them is crucial for the well-formedness of the sentence. Substituting for either of these noun phrases in such a way that they can not be associated with the reflexive causes a violation. For instance, if one substitutes for <u>his running mate</u> a first person pronoun, one obtains the ill-formed structure shown in (28).

    (28) *The incumbent told us that the convertion had nominated <u>themselves</u>

Much the same can be said about examples (26) and (27), which differ from (25) in that in them the sentential phrase containing the reflexive has a nominal rather than a verbal head. Among themselves (26) and (27) differ in that one has a lexical specifier but not the other.

Another property that sets apart those reflexives that must be associated with antecedent noun phrases that have the same sentential ancestry as they from those that may be associated with antecedents that do not have the same sentential ancestry as they concerns the relative linear order of reflexives and their antecedents. The antecedent noun phrases associated

with reflexives that have the same sentential ancestry as they
are necessarily to the left of the reflexives with which they
are associated. Those that are associated with reflexives
that do not have the same sentential ancestry as they, however,
need not be to the left of the reflexives in question. This
can be seen in examples (29)-(31).

(29) That the jury convicted himself disturbed
each defendent the most

(30) The jury's conviction of himself disturbed
each defendent the most

(31) That the picture of himself in the newspaper
is ugly enrages John

The antecedent associated with the reflexive in (29) is the
noun phrase each defendent. As one can see, the reflexive is
to the left of its antecedent. As with all sentences involving
reflexives, the well-formedness of (29) depends on the possibility
os associating the reflexive with an appropriate antecedent noun
phrase. Substituting for the antecedent of the reflexive a
noun phrase that can not be associated with it as its antecedent would cause a violation. If, for instance, one substitutes for the noun phrase each defendent, in (29) a plural
form of the same noun phrase, then one obtains an ill-formed

structure like the one shown in (32).

(32) *That the jury convicted <u>himself</u> disturbed the defendents the most

Much the same can be said about examples (30) and (31) which differ from example (29) in that the sentential phrase containing the reflexive has a nominal rather than a verbal head. Among themselves they differ with respect to the character of the specifier of this phrase.

In published discussions of this evidence, one can discern two approaches to the problems it poses. One denies the validity of the requirement that reflexives and their antecedents have the same sentential ancestry. The other does not challenge the validity of this requirement, but, instead, seeks to motivate a special reflexivization rule to account for those reflexives which do not conform to it. Recall that the particular significance of the earlier example (19) is that the reflexive and the noun phrase with which it is associated do not have the same sentential ancestry. While the embedded sentential phrase <u>The convention will nominate himself</u> contains the reflexive, it does not contain the noun phrase <u>each candidate</u> which is associated with it. Therefore, if one identifies the relation between the reflexive and this noun phrase as the relation between a reflexive and its grammatical antecedent, then one is forced to deny the validity of the claim that reflexives and their grammatical antecedents must have the same sentential ancestry. The approach Jackendoff takes to the question of the sentential ancestry of reflexives and their antecedents involves just this. Though he rejects the contention that reflexives and their antecedents must have the same sentential ancestry, he recognizes that there are certain conditions under which a reflexive can not be associated with an antecedent that does not have the same sentential ancestry as it does. For instance, if the reflexive in (19) did not have noun phrase stress, then it would not be possible to associate with it the subject of the matrix sentence as its antecedent, and, as a consequence, the sentence would be ill-formed. Jackendoff claims that a reflexive can be associated with an antecedent which does not have the same sentential ancestry as it, only if there is no potential grammatical antecedent that does have the same sentential ancestry. (A potential grammatical antecedent, as it will be remembered from Chapter Two, is any noun phrase that can function as the antecedent of some appropriate reflexive.) This can only occur if, among the noun phrases having the same sentential ancestry as

the reflexive, there is none that could be the antecedent of
some suitably chosen reflexive. Sentence (19), which represents a kind of sentence which Jackendoff did not take into
consideration, shows this claim to be false. The sentential
phrase embedded in (19) does contain a potential grammatical
antecedent in the form of its subject <u>the convention</u>. The
reflexive in the embedded sentential phrase can not be associated with an antecedent that does not have the same sentential ancestry as it does, because there is a potential
grammatical antecedent which has the same sentential ancestry
as the reflexive. Even though the potential grammatical antecedent is not appropriate, the reflexive is on Jackendoff's
analysis initially associated with it. Subsequently, when the
identity condition is enforced, the entire structure is rejected. Hence, the approach taken by Jackendoff fails to
account for well-formed sentences of the kind illustrated by
(19).

In fact, this kind of analysis does not only render invalid the condition that a reflexive and its grammatical antecedent must have the same sentential ancestry. It also invalidates a number of the other conditions on reflexives and
their grammatical antecedents that were established in Chapter

Two. The reason for this is that the noun phrases which, on this kind of analysis, are associated with reflexives as their grammatical antecedents do not all satisfy these conditions. For instance, it was shown in examples (25)-(27) that certain reflexives can be associated with antecedents consisting of several noun phrases that are not jointly analyzable as single constituents. If the antecedents associated with this kind of reflexive are identified as their grammatical antecedents, then one can not maintain the condition that valid antecedents of reflexives must be analyzable as single constituents. But this leaves one without an explanation for those cases where reflexives can not be associated with antecedent noun phrases which are not analyzable as single constituents.

The same goes for the requirement that the antecedent of a given reflexive must be to the left of the reflexive it is associated with. If the antecedents associated with the reflexives in examples (29)-(31) are identified as the grammatical antecedents of the reflexives in question, then it is no longer possible to uphold the validity of this requirement. On this analysis, the antecedents of the reflexives in (29)-(31) would be to the right rather than to the left of the reflexives they are associated with. As a consequence of this analysis, one would be left without an explanation for those cases where the antecedent of a reflexive must be to its left.

A different approach to the problem posed by the reflexives which are associated with noun phrases that do not have the same sentential ancestry as they is taken by Postal (1968a). In his monograph on so-called cross-over phenomena, he proposes to derive those reflexives that conform to the requirement that reflexives and their antecedents have the same sentential ancestry by one rule, and those that do not conform to it by another. This approach takes account of the fact that conditions on reflexives and the noun phrases with which they are associated differ in a number of points, depending on whether or not they have the same sentential ancestry. The reflexives derived by either of these two rules, however, have a number of properties in common. For instance, they do not differ in their morphology. But if they are derived independently of each other, then it is not at all necessary that they have any properties in common. In particular, they could just as well differ in their morphology. The fact of their independent derivation can only be interpreted as implying that the properties they share, they share as a matter of coincidence. While it is not easy to prove this implied claim false, a grammar that derives all reflexives by the same rule or rules is to be preferred over one that does not, because it makes a stronger claim. In such a grammar all reflexives necessarily have at least some properties in common.

In spite of this objection to two separate rules for deriving reflexives, one must not lose sight of the distinction of two kinds of reflexivization. Keeping in mind that both kinds of reflexivization have certain properties in common, one can see this distinction reflected in the fact that reflexives and the antecedent noun phrases with which they are associated satisfy different conditions depending on which kind of reflexivization they represent. Several such distinctions have already been discussed. In one case reflexives and the noun phrases with which they are associated must have the same sentential ancestry. In the other case this is not required. The antecedents of one kind must be analyzable as single constituents. In one case the noun phrases associated with the reflexives must be to their left. In the other case, this is not required.

There are, then, two cases to be considered. In one, reflexives and the noun phrases with which they are associated satisfy certain particular conditions; in the other, they

satisfy certain others. The conditions that characterize
one case are in conflict with the conditions that characterize
the other, though there are conditions that are common to both
cases. The conflict can obviously not be resolved by requiring
that only those conditions which both cases have in common can
be satisfied, because this would underspecify the set of well-
formed sentences involving reflexives. Nor can the conflict
be resolved by treating the two cases of reflexivization as entirely separate phenomena, because this does not take account
of the conditions that are common to both. One can account
for both the differences and the similarities, however, in the
following way. In the case of the examples of Chapter Two, the
reflexives are associated with antecedent noun phrases in terms
of certain conditions. In the case of the examples of Chapter
Two, the reflexives are associated with antecedent noun phrases
in terms of certain conditions. In the case of the examples
under consideration here, one could postulate underlying
structures containing appropriate noun phrases with which the
reflexives could be associated in terms of the conditions that
are satisfied by the examples of Chapter Two. This would
account for the properties that both cases have in common. The
difference between the two cases would then be expressed by the

fact that in one case, but not in the other, the reflexives are also associated with another noun phrase in terms of certain other conditions.

The fact that the reflexives in question have noun phrase stress suggest that in the underlying structure they should be represented as emphatic reflexives, the antecedents of which are supplied in accordance with this proposal. A sentence like (19) would, on this analysis, derive from the underlying structure represented informally as (33).

>(33) Each candidate hopes the convention will nominate him *himself*

That the reflexive in (19) has noun phrase stress is accounted for by this analysis by deriving it, the reflexive, from an emphatic reflexive. Indeed, the noun phrase stress on the reflexive in (19) may be considered evidence for the derivation of (19) from (33). Regarding the stress on reflexives which on this analysis are derived from emphatic reflexives the antecedents of which have been deleted, it has been noted above that those reflexives that are constituents of sentential phrases with nominal heads the specifiers of which are not lexical need not have noun phrase stress. These reflexives may have pronominal stress or noun phrase stress. By themselves, the examples in which the reflexives under consideration have pronominal stress provide no evidence for the proposed analysis. Corresponding to each of these examples here, however, is one in which the reflexive has noun phrase stress. These examples, of course, do support the proposed analysis. It is logically possible that the examples in which the reflexives have pronominal stress are derived by a process that is completely different from the process by which the corresponding examples in which the reflexives have noun phrase stress are derived in accordance with the proposed analysis. It is much more plausible, however, that the examples with pronominal stress are derived in the same way as those with noun phrase stress except for the difference in the stress assigned to the reflexive. This difference in stress could be the result of stress reduction. One might argue, for instance, that a sentential phrase whose specifier is not lexical can be reanalyzed as a noun phrase and that as a result of this reanalysis other stress rules become applicable. The operation of each of these rules (insofar as it does not assign stress to the reflexive itself) would cause the stress on the reflexive to be reduced by one degree. In this way it would be possible for noun phrase stress on the reflexive to be reduced to pronominal stress. This would account for the fact that in sentential phrases with nominal heads and non-lexical specifiers such as (23), (27) and (31) the reflexives in question may have either pronominal stress or noun phrase stress. In addition, it explains why in sentential phrases with nominal heads and lexical specifiers and in sentential phrases with verbal heads the reflexives in question may not have pronominal stress. Such sentential phrases are not subject to a reanalysis as noun phrases and as a consequence the stress on the reflexives in question can not be reduced.

The well-formedness of (19), after the grammatical antecedent of the reflexive in the underlying structure has been deleted, depends on the possibility of associating the reflexive with some appropriate noun phrase in terms of certain conditions which were discussed above. One can ensure that these conditions are satisfied if one makes the possibility of deleting this pronoun conditional on the possibility of associating it with an appropriate noun phrase. Indeed, this is not a condition on the transformation that deletes pronouns in front of reflexives alone. The same condition is met by the complement subject deletion rule. Hence, this condition can be extracted from the statement of particular rules and stated as part of

the theory of grammar. That there is a condition on the
deletion of noun phrases which links the possibility of deletion and the possibility of associating the constituent to
be deleted with an appropriate antecedent has been thoroughly
documented by Postal (1968b). In his study of complement
subject deletion he has noted that in a number of points the
conditions under which complement subjects can be deleted
are the same as the conditions under which anaphoric pronouns
can be associated with antecedents. Consider, for example,
sentence (34).

  (34) His finding out that Greta was a vampire
     worried somebody

In example (34) the indefinite noun phrase somebody in the
object of the matrix sentence can not be associated with the
pronoun his in the subject of the complement phrase as its antecedent. As a rule the indefinite noun phrase somebody is an
appropriate antecedent for the pronoun his. As S.-Y. Kuroda
first observed, however, it is not possible to associate an
anaphoric pronoun with an indefinite antecedent noun phrase
that it to its right. This accounts for the fact that in (34)
somebody can not be the antecedent of the pronoun his. Postal
notes that this same condition can be made to account for the

ill-formedness of sentence (35) if the possibility of associating a given complement subject with an appropriate antecedent is made a precondition on its deletion.

(35) *Finding out Greta was a vampire worried somebody

Inasmuch as the possibility of associating a given complement subject with an appropriate antecedent is a precondition on its deletion, the fact that this can not be done in (34) accounts for the ill-formedness of (35).

On the positive side, on the assumption that the possibility of deleting a given complement subject depends on the possibility of associating it with an appropriate antecedent, it is a natural consequence of the fact that in (36) the subject of the complement phrase can be associated with an antecedent that it can be deleted.

(36) John argued with me about our shaving ourselves

In example (36) the noun phrase *John* and the pronominal noun phrase *me* can be associated with the pronoun *our* in the subject of the complement phrase as its antecedent. The complement subject therefore satisfies the hypothesized precondition on the possibility of deleting complement subjects. Consequently, in the absense of any independent restriction on complement subject deletion it can be deleted, as one can see in example

(37).

(37) John argued with me about shaving ourselves

But for the fact that the complement subject in (36) is associated with an antecedent that is not analyzable as a single constituent, the possibility of deleting it in the derivation of (37) may not seem remarkable. The possibility of deleting a complement subject under the conditions illustrated by the derivation of sentence (37) for the structure underlying (36) has been largely ignored. Indeed, such a derivation poses insuperable difficulties for the minimal distance principle of Rosenbaum (1965, 1967), because it is only defined between two nodes and not three. The possibility of derivations like that of sentence (37), however, is quite compatible with the assumption that the possibility of deleting complement subjects depends on the possibility of associating them with appropriate antecedents, since it is quite generally possible to associate free (though not bound) anaphoric pronouns with antecedents that are not analyzable as single constituents.

Similarly the fact that the subject of the most deeply embedded complement in sentence (38) can be associated with an appropriate antecedent that one can derive from the structure underlying (38), a sentence in which this constituent has been deleted, is consistent with the assumption that the possibility of deleting a complement subject depends on the possibility of associating it with an appropriate antecedent.

(38) The young lady thinks that it is difficult for her to hurt herself

In example (38) the noun phrase _the young lady_ in the subject of the matrix sentence can be associated with the pronoun _her_ in the subject of the complement phrase _for her to hurt herself_. as its antecedent. This satisfies the proposed condition on complement subject deletion. Since nothing else stands in the way of deleting the constituent in question it is possible to derive the sentence shown in (39) by doing so.

(39) The young lady thinks that it is difficult to hurt herself

The antecedent associated with the deleted complement subject is the subject of the matrix sentence _The young lady thinks that S_. Embedded in place of the S in the matrix sentence is the sentential phrase _it is difficult S_. This phrase separates the phrase containing the antecedent of the complement subject from the complement phrase itself, which is embedded in it in place of the S. Within the context of past work on complementation, it is remarkable that in the derivation of sentence (39) the

deleted complement subject and the antecedent noun phrase
with which it is associated should be separated by an intervening sentential phrase. There is nothing surprising, however, about the fact that two noun phrases one of which is the antecedent of the other should be separated in this way. Hence, the possibility of a derivation like that of sentence (39) is quite compatible with the assumption that the possibility of deleting complement subjects depends on the possibility of associating them with appropriate antecedents.

Returning to the question of deriving certain reflexives from emphatic reflexives by deleting their antecedents, one finds that as in the case of the deletion of complement subjects this deletion operation depends on the possibility of associating the deleted constituents with appropriate antecedents. On the assumption that the reflexive in (25) derives from an emphatic reflexive, the structure underlying this sentence would be (40).

(40) The incumbent told his running mate that the convention had nominated them themselves

The fact that the reflexive in (25) has noun phrase stress can be related to the fact that in the structure underlying (25) it is an emphatic reflexive. It is possible to delete the antecedent of the emphatic reflexive in the derivation of (25).

because it can be associated with an appropriate antecedent which, in this case, happens to consist of two noun phrases that can not be analyzed as a single constituent.

As a last example the underlying structure that one arrives at for sentence (30) if the reflexive in it is derived from an emphatic reflexive can be represented as (41).

>(41) The jury's conviction of him <u>himself</u> disturbed each defendent the most

By deriving (30) from the structure represented in (41), one can account for the fact that the reflexive in (30) has noun phrase stress because it is an emphatic reflexive in its underlying structure. It is possible to associate the antecedent of this reflexive with an appropriate antecedent of its own, and, hence, it is possible to delete it.

The rule that deletes the grammatical antecedents of emphatic reflexives provides yet another way of deriving reflexives from underlying emphatic reflexives. Because of the possibilities that the derivation of reflexives from emphatic reflexives opens up, it is necessary to examine the limitations imposed on the operation of this rule. Consider, for example, the ill-formed sentence shown in (42).

>(42) *The jury's conviction of <u>himself</u> disturbed, somebody the most

Sentence (42) is identical to (30) except that in place of the noun phrase <u>each defendent</u> in the object of the matrix sentence, sentence (42) has the indefinite noun phrase <u>somebody</u>. Correspondingly, sentence (42) would have to have an underlying structure that differed from the structure underlying (30) in only this point. Such a structure is given in (43).

(43) The jury's conviction of him <u>himself</u> disturbed somebody the most

Given the underlying structure represented in (43), sentence (42) can not be derived from it, because it is not possible to associate the antecedent of the reflexive with an appropriate antecedent noun phrase. In particular, it can not be associated with the indefinite noun phrase <u>somebody</u> because a pronoun can only be associated with an indefinite antecedent if the antecedent is to its left. In view of this, no special conditions need be imposed on the rule that deletes pronouns preceding emphatic reflexives in order to prevent derivations such as this.

Or consider the undesirable possibility of deriving a sentence like <u>The rich hate themselves</u> from an underlying structure like <u>The rich hate them themselves</u> by deleting the antecedent of the emphatic reflexive. Such a derivation is undesirable because it competes with the derivation established in Chapter Two making one of the two possible derivations superfluous. It is not a possible derivation because the noun phrase the rich in the subject of this sentence can not be associated with the antecedent of the reflexive as its antecedent.

The possibility of deriving reflexives from emphatic reflexives opens up the possibility of deriving reflexives in subject position. Take, for instance, the structure underlying sentence (44).

(44) The incumbent knows that he himself can't win

Since it is possible to associate the noun phrase the incumbent in the subject of the matrix sentence with the pronoun he preceding the reflexive in the subject of the embedded sentential phrase, one might expect the rule deleting pronouns before reflexives to apply. If it did apply, it would derive the ill-formed structure given in (45).

(45) *The incumbent knows that himself can't win

In spite of the fact that the pronoun can be associated with an appropriate antecedent, however, it can not be deleted because of the condition that prohibits the deletion of the subject of an embedded sentential phrase which has that as a complementizer. As Perlmutter (1968) has stated, this condition is applied only to the deletion of the entire subject noun phrase. There seems to be no reason, however, not to state it in such a way that it applies to the deletion of the head of the complement subject. Formulated in this way, this condition prohibits the deletion of the entire subject noun phrase as well. Again, no conditions need be imposed on the rule deleting pronouns before emphatic reflexives. Its proper operation is ensured by conditions that are part of the theory of grammar. There may, however, be other environments in which the antecedent of an emphatic reflexive in the subject of an embedded sentential phrase may be deleted. Consider, for instance, the structure given schematically in (46) with the embedded sentential phrase enclosed in square brackets.

(46) Each candidate expects for him himself to win

Assuming that in the environment of (46) it is possible to delete the pronoun preceding the reflexive, then it might be possible to derive sentence (47) from this structure.

(47) Each candidate expects himself to win

If this analysis can be substantiated, then it might well be possible to do away with the analysis based on the subject raising transformation.

Therefore, consider the two sentences (47) and (48) side by side.

(48) Each candidate expects him to win

It is generally agreed that the structures underlying (47) and (48) are identical except for the subject of the embedded sentential complement phrase. The deep structure of either of these sentences consists of the matrix sentence Each candidate expects S where S stands for a sentential phrase of the form (for) X to win. The constituent X is the subject of the sentential complement, and the two sentences differ with respect to the lexical item that makes up this constituent. It is widely assumed that in the surface structure of these sentences, X, the underlying complement subject, is no longer a constituent of the sentential complement. In particular, it is assumed that in the course of the derivation of these sentences a transformational rule, variously called pronoun replacement, it replacement, or raising, applies to extract the complement subject from the sentential complement so that in the surface structure it is not a constituent of the complement. On this analysis, the surface structure of sentences (47) and (48) can be schematically represented as a matrix of the form Each candidate expects X S where the S-node dominates what is left of the

embedded sentential complement, (for) to win. In support of
this claim, it has been pointed out that as a result of
passivization the underlying subject of the complement
sentence may in the surface structure be the derived subject
of the matrix sentence. For example, when the structure underlying sentence (48) is passivized, one obtains sentence (49).

(49) He is expected to win by each candidate

In the structure underlying (48) and (49) the third person
pronoun in the subject of the matrix sentence in (49) is the
subject of the sentential complement (for) X to win. In the
surface structure of (49) it is, of course, no longer a constituent of the complement. It is generally assumed that in
the derivation of (49) the underlying complement subject is
extracted from the complement prior to passivization. But the
passivization process, as it is usually formulated, applies to
any sentence that can be analyzed as NP-V-NP, whether or not
the constituent NP that follows the constituent V is in an
embedded sentential complement. Nor is there any reason to
require that this noun phrase not be in an embedded sentential
complement. Therefore, the fact that the structure underlying
(48) and (49) may undergo this process is no evidence for the
hypothesis that there is a transformation that extracts the

subjects of certain sentential complements. The fact that in the surface structure the underlying subject of the sentential complement in examples like (48) has the form of an object pronoun has also been advanced as an argument to show that in the surface structure what was the complement subject has been extracted from the complement. In effect, it is argued, that the former complement subject is substituted in the matrix sentence in object position, and that it is for this reason that it has object form. But this evidence again fails to make the point it is intended to make. The subjects of all infinitival complements have object form insofar as this form can be distinguished from subject form. This is readily apparent in a sentence like <u>It is too cold for them to swim</u> in which the pronoun <u>them</u> in the subject of the sentential complement can not be analyzed as an object in the matrix sentence. Indeed, the corresponding sentence with the subject of the sentential complement in subject form is ill-formed: <u>It is too cold for they to swim</u>. Often the fact that in examples like (47) the constituent X is a reflexive, <u>himself</u> in this case, that has associated with it as an antecedent the subject of the matrix sentence, <u>each candidate </u>in this case, is cited as support for the contention that the underlying complement subject is in the surface structure no longer a constituent of the sentential complement. Since the subject of the matrix sentence is associated with the reflexive as its antecedent, the reasoning goes, it must be the case that the subject of the matrix sentence and the reflexive have the same sentential ancestry. Since the subject of the matrix sentence is not dominated by the embedded sentential complement, this can only be the case if the reflexive is not a constituent of the complement. But the constituent X, the superficial reflexive, is the underlying complement subject. Therefore, this constituent must have been extracted from the complement. This argument, however, is inconclusive also. In the surface structure reflexives and the antecedent noun phrases with which they were associated at the point of their derivation need not have the same sentential ancestry. Hence, the fact that a reflexive is associating with a particular antecedent noun phrase is by itself no indication of the sentential ancestry of the reflexive.

As in the case of reflexives, the well-formedness of a sentence involving a reciprocal depends on the possibility of associating the reciprocal with an appropriate antecedent. In particular, it is not possible for a reciprocal to be derived unless it can be associated with an antecedent noun phrase that has the same sentential ancestry as it does. To see how this can be accounted for it is necessary to understand how reciprocals are introduced into a sentence. A reciprocal may be analyzed as a noun phrase in which the distributive quantifier _each_ is followed by the noun _other_ just as in the noun phrase _each candidate_ the quantifier _each_ is followed by the noun _candidate_. According to the insightful analysis of reciprocals of Dougherty (1968), reciprocals differ from other noun phrases with the distributive quantifier in that the distributive quantifier is not present in the underlying representation of reciprocals. Rather, the form of the noun phrase underlying a reciprocal is either _the other_ or _the others_. In the underlying structure the quantifier is associated with the antecedent of the reciprocal. The reciprocal proper is produced transformationally by removing the quantifier from the antecedent and substituting it for the determiner in the noun phrase underlying the reciprocal. This transformational procedure relates the structure underlying a sentence like _Each candidate attacked the other_ to the structure underlying the sentence _The candidates attacked each other_, and these sentences are indeed synonymous. The operation of this procedure is limited in much the same way as the operation of the copying procedure involved in the derivation of reflexives is. The details of this were given in Chapter Two. In this way it is ensured that at the point of its derivation a reciprocal and its antecedent must have the same sentential ancestry.

There are other formulations of the procedure to derive reciprocals that differ from this one; however, it is generally agreed that reciprocals are derived by a transformational or a quasi-transformational process and that at the point of their derivation reciprocals must be associated with antecedent noun phrases that have the same sentential ancestry as they. Now, if in the derivation of sentences of the kind illustrated by (47) and (48) the complement subject is extracted from the complement to yield a structure of the form Each candidate expects X S in which the noun phrase each candidate, the subject of the matrix sentence, and X have the same sentential ancestry, then one would expect to find a sentence in which X is a reciprocal which has the subject of the matrix sentence associated with it as its antecedent. Sentence (50), if it were well-formed, would be an example of this kind.

(50) *The candidates expected each other to clash

If the reciprocal in sentence (50) were derived from the underlying complement subject the others after it has been extracted from the complement, then there could be no obstacle to deriving a reciprocal in this example. The assumption that the subject of a complement sentence may under certain conditions be extracted from the complement leads one to predict, incorrectly, that sentence is well-formed. Hence, the fact that this sentence is not well-formed contradicts the contention that there is a special rule that extracts complement subjects from the complement phrase. This is not to say that complement subjects may not under any circumstances be extracted from the complement phrase. Indeed, in example (49) it was shown that the passivization process may do so. In this regard, the operation of the rule of passivization is similar to that of the rule of WH-fronting. In view of the evidence showing that the subject of the complement in sentences like (47) has not been raised, the reflexives in these examples can not be handled in the manner outlined in Chapter Two. Instead, one may propose for them an analysis along the lines of this discussion, deriving them from emphatic reflexives, the grammatical antecedents of which are deleted. On this analysis, sentence (47) does indeed derive from the structure shown in (46). By deriving the reflexive in (47) from an emphatic reflexive, one accounts for the fact that it has noun phrase

stress. (That noun phrase stress is not necessary and that
pronominal stress is possible will be considered a result of
stress reduction.) The fact that in a sentence such as Each
candidate expected to win the complement subject can be deleted
shows that the complement subject can be associated with an
appropriate antecedent. Hence, it must also be possible to
associate the grammatical antecedent of an emphatic reflexive
in the complement subject of a sentence like (46) with an
appropriate antecedent and consequently to delete it. Indeed,
it seems that this deletion is obligatory. The fact that the
reflexive in (47) derives from an emphatic reflexive associated
with the complement subject can be verified directly in sentences
like (51) where the reflexive is preceded by the complementizer
which marks the beginning of the complement phrase.

(51) What each candidate expects is for himself
to win

By deleting a complement subject that is the grammatical
antecedent of an emphatic reflexive without deleting the reflexive too, reflexives can be derived in complement subject
position. This possibility, if it is not appropriately restricted, gives rise to undesirable derivations. For instance,
it is generally agreed that a sentence like Each candidate tried

to win derives from an underlying structure that may be schematically represented as the matrix sentence Each candidate tried S where S stands for an embedded sentential phrase of the form (for)X to win. In this particular case, the constituent X in the subject of the complement phrase is such that in thepresence of the noun phrase each candidate in the subject of the matrix sentence it can be deleted. In fact, it is necessarily such that it can be deleted. Conceivably, it would be possible to associate an emphatic reflexive with any complement subject, in particular one that must be deleted obligatorily. And by deleting the complement subject but not the reflexive one would derive a sentence with a reflexive in place of the complement subject. Thus, from an underlying structure of the form Each candidate tried for X himself to win one would derive the ill-formed sentence shown in (52).

(52) *Each candidate tried for himself to win

One can prevent such sentences from being derived by not allowing those complement subjects that are deleted obligatorily to be associated with emphatic reflexives as their antecedents.

It has been noted earlier that under certain conditions the antecedent of an emphatic reflexive can be deleted when it is a first or second person subject pronoun but not otherwise.

While in general it is possible to delete the antecedent of an emphatic reflexive only if it can be associated with an appropriate antecedent of its own, when the antecedent is a first or a second person subject pronoun then it can be deleted even if it is (apparently) not associated with an antecedent. It has been argued above that in addition to the rule that deletes the antecedent of an emphatic reflexive if it can be associated with an appropriate antecedent, there is another rule that can delete the antecedent of an emphatic reflexive independently of the possibility of associating it with an appropriate antecedent, if it is either a first or a second person subject pronoun. There may indeed be derivations in which either rule is defined and either rule may apply. According to a proposal of Ross (1968=1970), however, there is only one rule to delete the antecedent of emphatic reflexives. Ross too envisions the possibility of deleting the antecedent of an emphatic reflexive if it can be associated with an appropriate antecedent, but he does not provide for the deletion of antecedents of emphatic reflexives that can not be associated with antecedents of their own. Rather, he analyses those examples in which there does not appear to be an antecedent associated with a deleted constituent of this kind as deriving

from underlying structures in which there is one. In
support of this contention Ross offers certain sentences in
the derivation of which the antecedent of an emphatic reflexive has been deleted. Each sentence in which the deleted
constituent can be associated with an appropriate antecedent
can, according to Ross, be matched up with a similar sentence
in which it does not appear possible to do this. Some of these
sentences are well-formed, others ill-formed. In addition,
Ross distinguishes at least two degrees of acceptability intermediate between well-formedness and ill-formedness among
the sentences he cites.

In the structure underlying the sentence <u>Tom believed
that he himself had written the paper</u> it is possible to associate the antecedent of the emphatic reflexive with an antecedent of its own, namely the subject noun phrase <u>Tom</u>.
Sentence (53), the sentence derived by deleting this antecedent noun phrase, is nevertheless ill-formed.

      (53) *Tom believed that himself had written the paper

According to Ross this sentence is matched by the sentence
<u>I myself wrote this paper</u> in which the antecedent of an emphatic reflexive can not apparently be associated with an

antecedent of its own. As one can see from example (54) the
sentence derived by deleting the antecedent of the emphatic
reflexive is again ill-formed.

(54) *Myself wrote this paper

Whether or not the antecedent can be associated with an antecedent of its own, the derivation yields an ill-formed sentence in either case. Ross considers a number of other matching pairs of examples of this kind and in each case judges both examples to be of the same degree of acceptability. From this he concludes: "Whatever the rule is that produces the complex spectrum of acceptabilities in (the case of examples where the deleted constituent can be associated with an antecedent of its own , it is obvious that the same rule is in operation in the case of such apparently simple sentences as those in which the deleted constituent can not be associated with an antecedent of its own ." Granting that sentences (53) and (54) are ill-formed for the same reason, it simply does not follow that they are ill-formed because the same rule has misapplied. They may, for instance, be ill-formed because two different rules have applied in violation of the same principle. It has, for instance, been shown in the course of the discussion of examples (44) and (45) that the impossibility of deleting the antecedent of an emphatic reflexive in the subject of a complement phrase that is introduced by the complementizer <u>that</u> as in the case of example (53) can be related to the impossibility of deleting the subject of such complement phrases. If this is the proper explanation for the fact that the antecedent of the emphatic reflexive in the subject of sentence (53) can not be deleted then one can apply this explanation to sentence (54) by deriving it from an underlying structure in which this sentence is introduced by a that complementizer. This proposal is not unreasonable. While in English it might appear that the presence of a complementizer is what distinguishes an embedded sentential phrase from one that is not embedded, if one looks at other languages one finds examples of sentences that are not embedded that do have complementizers. Ross himself notes one in his section 2.2.3., the complementizer <u>?inna</u> in Arabic.

The discovery that there are similar restrictions on the deletion of the antecedents of emphatic reflexives when they can and when they can not be associated with appropriate antecedents of their own is no evidence for the contention that the deletion is achieved by one and the same transformational process. It is this contention, however, that Ross cites in support of the so-called performative analysis. According to this analysis each surface structure sentence is derived from a deep structure in which it is embedded in a sentence with a first person singular subject, a performative verb, and a second person object. The observation that certain first and second person pronouns that are antecedents of emphatic reflexives can be deleted apparently without there being any antecedents associated with them in conjunction with the contention that the pronouns in question can only be deleted if they are associated with antecedents would indeed constitute evidence for the underlying first and second person pronouns that the performative analysis presupposes, if this contention could be substantiated. The possibility of deleting a constituent if it can be associated with some other constituent, however, does not imply that if a constituent can be deleted, then it is possible to associate it with some other constituent. By the same token, the performative analysis, if it could be substantiated, would constitute evidence for the contention that the antecedent of an emphatic reflexive can only be deleted if it can be associated with an appropriate antecedent of its own. This analysis provides antecedents for those cases where these constituents can be deleted apparently even without being associated with appropriate antecedents. It is, therefore, appropriate to consider further evidence bearing on the validity of this analysis. Consider, for instance, a sentence such as (55).

(55) The whole family, we ourselves included, will go to the beach

On the assumption of the performative analysis, sentence (55) in its underlying structure is embedded in a performative sentence. Informally speaking, one might say that sentence (55) is embedded in place of the S in a sentence somewhat like I say to you that S. The pronoun we in the antecedent of the emphatic reflexive in sentence (55) can not be associated with an antecedent. (It could possibly be associated with the subject and the object of the performative sentence jointly but this would limit one to an inclusive interpretation of this pronoun.) If one were to assume the performative analysis as it stands and it one were also to assume that the antecedent of an emphatic reflexive can only be deleted if it can be associated with an antecedent of its own, then it would not be possible to delete the antecedent of the emphatic reflexive in sentence (55) because it would not be possible to associate it with an appropriate antecedent. This analysis would therefore fail to generate the well-formed sentence (56).

> (56) The whole family, ourselves included, will go to the beach

According to the alternate analysis advanced in this chapter, however, this sentence can be generated in the same manner as sentences (13) and (14). According to this analysis the antecedent of an emphatic reflexive may be deleted without being associated with an antecedent of its own if it is a first or second person subject pronoun. The derivation of sentence (58) is analagous to the derivation of sentence (13) except that the deleted pronoun is in the plural rather than in the singular.

NOTES

1. For those who have difficulty with regard to the acceptability of this example, it might facilitate understanding to point out that it answers the question <u>Who does each candidate hope the convention will nominate</u> on the assumption that candidate A hopes the convention will nominate candidate A, etc.

CHAPTER FOUR

This chapter deals with the meaning of reflexives in relation to the meaning of their antecedents. The notion meaning, as it is understood here, has at least two distinct distinct aspects: following Frege (1892), these are sense and reference. For present purposes it will be assumed that there are no others. Putting it in these terms the subject matter of this chapter is the sense of reflexives in relation to the sense of their antecedents and the reference of reflexives in relation to the reference of their antecedents. To see what this means it is necessary to know what is meant by the terms sense and reference, or at least what is meant by the sense or the reference of a noun or noun phrase. The sense of a noun is its dictionary definition. In one form or another this information is a part of the lexical entry of a noun along with information about its phonological and syntactic properties. The reference of a noun is the object which the noun designates, where it is understood that a noun may not have reference. The sense of a noun that has reference amounts to a statement of the criteria (properties) that an object must satisfy in order for the noun to apply to it. Reference is, of course, in part a function of sense. A given noun can not designate an object that does not meet the criteria (satisfy the properties) set forth in the statement of the sense of that noun. The noun in question can not have such an object as its reference. Take, for example, the noun husband. This noun can only apply to a man; it can not apply to a woman. Hence, the reference of this noun can only be a man and not a woman.

To be sure, this chapter is not concerned with meaning as such but with the meaning of one noun phrase in relation to the meaning of another. Therefore, to simplify matters, the discussion will be limited to examples in which the difference between the meaning of a given noun phrase and the meaning of its head noun can safely be ignored. Insofar as there are restrictive modifiers, demonstratives, or quantifiers associated with a noun phrase, its meaning is not the same as the meaning of its head noun. For example, restrictive modifiers may add to the criteria that an object must satisfy in order for a given noun phrase to apply to it. As a consequence the sense of a noun phrase involving a restrictive modifier will differ from the sense of its head noun and this will have a corresponding effect on the reference of this noun phrase. Take, for example, the noun spouse. It can apply to a man as well as to a woman. Consider, however, the noun phrase <u>male spouse</u> in which the restrictive modifier <u>male</u> is associated with the noun <u>spouse</u>. This noun phrase can only apply to a man and not to a woman. The restrictive modifier <u>male</u> has, in effect, added a criterion to the statement of the sense of the noun phrase <u>male spouse</u> which is not a part of the sense of its head noun <u>spouse</u>.

The sense of two different nouns may partially coincide, as, for example, in the case of the nouns <u>husband</u> and <u>wife</u>. One has the sense of male spouse and the other the sense of female spouse. The sense of (the noun) <u>spouse</u> is common to both. The sense of these two nouns differs in that one can only apply to a man and the other only to a woman. Each of the criteria in the statement of the sense of a given noun may in effect be thought of as a binary feature, which may be marked either positively or negatively or else not marked at all. Whenever a noun is marked either positively or negatively for a given feature, then it applies only to objects that positively or negatively satisfy the criterion for which that feature stands. Whenever a noun is not marked for a given feature, then it applies to objects irrespective of the criterion in question. Putting it this way the nouns <u>husband</u> and <u>wife</u> have the same markings for the features that they share with the noun *spouse*. They have opposite markings for at least one feature, the feature that stands for the criterion of sex. Inasmuch as there is at least one feature in the statement of the sense of these nouns for which one is marked positively and the other negatively, these nouns have opposite sense.

Two different nouns may not have the same sense and yet not have opposite sense. Consider, for example, the nouns *husband* and *father*. The criteria that an object must meet in order for the noun *husband* to apply to it are not the same criteria that an object must meet in order for the noun *father* to apply. Hence, the noun *husband* and the noun *father* do not have the same sense. It is possible, however, for an object to meet both the criteria for the noun *husband* and the noun *father* so that both nouns would apply to it. Neither of these two nouns is marked positively for a feature for which the other is marked negatively. There is no criterion that must be satisfied positively if one of these nouns is to apply and that must be satisfied negatively if the other is to apply.

The meaning of two noun phrases may be related because either their sense or their reference is related. There can not be a significant relation between the meaning of one noun phrase and the meaning of another, if neither their sense nor

their reference is related. One kind of meaningful relation
between noun phrases exists when they have the same meaning.
Take, for instance, a sentence like (1).

    (1)   Once there was a king and the king had a
           lovely daughter

In (1) the noun phrase <u>a king</u> and the noun phrase <u>the king</u>
both have the same sense. Both apply to a male royal sovereign.
In addition, as sentence (1) is normally understood, these two
noun phrases identify one and the same king and hence have the
same reference. The two noun phrases in question have the same
sense and the same reference and, hence, the same meaning.
But two noun phrases may be related in a meaningful way when
they have the same sense and not the same reference or the
same reference and not the same sense. Consider, for example,
sentence (2).

    (2)   After building us a house you built yourself
           a house

The two occurrences of the noun phrase <u>a house</u> in sentence (2)
have the same sense. The two occurrences of this noun can not
be understood, however, as identifying the same house. Hence,
they do not have the same reference. What is significant about
the relation between the meaning of the noun phrases in question

is that they have the same sense, though they do not have the same reference. Following this example of two noun phrases having the same sense but not the same reference, consider an example of two noun phrases that have the same reference but not the same sense. Such an example, originally cited by Chomsky (1969), is given in (3).

(3) I am not against my father, (I am) only against the labor minister

When this sentence is spoken by the son of the labor minister (as it was by the son of the Brasilian labor minister), then the noun phrase my father and the noun phrase the labor minister have the same reference. Both identify the same person. The criteria by which this person is identified by the noun phrase my father are different, however, from the criteria by which the same person is identified by the noun phrase the labor minister. One noun phrase identifies this person as the father of the speaker of (3) and the other as the official holding the position of labor minister. Though these two noun phrases differ in sense, their meaning is related because they have the same reference.

Notice, furthermore, that the noun phrases my father and the labor minister which, as they are used in sentence (3),

have the same reference though not the same sense, nevertheless
do not have opposite sense. It is, indeed, a general rule that
two noun phrases having opposite sense can not be understood as
having the same reference. If, for instance, one were to substitute for the noun phrase the labor minister in sentence (3)
the noun phrase my mother, which has the opposite sense of the
noun phrase my father, one would obtain the sentence given in
(4).

(4) I am not against my father, I am only against
my mother

The two noun phrases my father and my mother in sentence (4)
can not be understood as having the same reference.

The transformational theory of reflexivization assumes
that reflexives and their antecedents have the same sense and
the same reference. Or, in other words, all formulations of
this theory agree on the assumption that the sense of a given
reflexive or the form underlying it is given in the base, so
that it can be determined from the deep structure of the
sentence in which the reflexive occurs. As this theory of
reflexivization is usually formulated, this is implicit in
the fact that the underlying representation of a reflexive
and that of its antecedent consist of the same lexical item.

Part of those lexical items is, of course, the statement of the criteria that an object must satisfy in order for the particular lexical item to apply to it, which is, of course, the sense of that lexical item. The statement of Jackendoff's cited in Chapter Two is open to interpretation. In particular, it can be interpreted as claiming that coreferential noun phrases (and reflexives and their antecedents are assumed to be coreferential noun phrases) must agree in their semantic properties which would mean that they must have the same sense. The phrase structure theory of reflexivization does not agree with this, but this question will be taken up later.

Some formulations of the transformational theory of reflexivization assume that in addition to the sense of a reflexive its reference (relative to other noun phrases) is also given in the base, so that it too can be determined from the deep structure of the sentence in which the reflexive occurs. For instance, Postal (1966b), following Chomsky (1965), assigns each noun or noun phrase that is entered into the deep structure of a sentence an integer as an index. The particular integer chosen for an index is in general arbitrary though for first and second person pronouns it is fixed. The interpretation of these indices is such that sameness of index stands for sameness

of reference and difference of index stands for difference
of reference. (The indices themselves do not indicate
reference as such.) The reflexivization as well as the pronominalization processes are sensitive to these indices. In
particular, a given pair of noun phrases that is otherwise
subject to the reflexivization process can undergo reflexivization only if both have the same index or, in other words,
the same reference. What is more, Postal contends that any
such pair of noun phrases must undergo reflexivization.
Whenever two noun phrases have the same sense and the same
reference (expressed by the sameness of their indices) and
otherwise satisfy the conditions on the reflexivization
process, then, on Postal's analysis a reflexive is substituted
for one. Consideration of example (5), however, shows that
this conception of the reflexivization process can not be
the correct one.

(5) Violence begets violence

The two occurrences of the noun phrase *violence* in sentence
(5), once as a subject noun phrase and once as an object noun
phrase, have the same sentential ancestry. It is not possible
to understand the reference of one as being one violence and
the reference of the other another violence. Hence, both have

the same reference. Both consist of the same lexical item, hence, both have the same sense. Since both occurrences of the noun phrase <u>violence</u> have the same sense and the same reference and satisfy all other conditions that apply to the reflexivization process, a reflexive would on Postal's analysis have to be substituted for one, and it would not be possible to generate sentence (5) as it is. Other formulations of the transformational theory of reflexivization do not run into this difficulty. The reflexivization process as it is formulated by Lees and Klima (1963) is optional in the third person. This has generally been interpreted as meaning that whenever two noun phrases that have the same sentential ancestry fail to undergo reflexivization, then they do not have the same reference. But no such claim is to be found in the paper of Lees and Klima (1963). Therefore, sentence (5) can be accounted for by simply omitting reflexivization. On Jackendoff's analysis, reflexives are bona fide lexical items. Like all lexical items they are inserted directly into base structures. The choice of one lexical item over another is, of course, free, all other things being equal. On this analysis, the lexical item chosen to fill the object position in sentence (5) just happens to be the same as the lexical item filling the subject position. This poses no problem whatsoever.

Much the same goes for the phrase structure theory of reflexivization, only here reflexives are not unanalyzable lexical items but rather restricted possessives with the head noun _self_. All other things being equal, the choice of a particular lexical item to fill a particular lexical category is free, in particular, the choice of a restricted possessive with the head noun _self_ is optional.

Returning to the question of the reference of reflexives as it is handled by different formulations of the transformational theory of reflexivization. Lees and Klima are not explicit on this point, but rather take it for granted that a reflexive and its antecedent have the same reference. An interesting question remains. What is the reference of the underlying representation of a reflexive? Does it have the same reference as the antecedent of the reflexive? If it does and if it is the reflexive alone that has the same reference as its antecedent, then the reflexivization process would contribute to the meaning of the sentence contrary to the assumptions of the standard theory.

Indeed, in Jackendoff's formulation there are certain

noun phrases such as reflexives, anaphoric pronouns, and pronominal epithets such as <u>that bum</u> of which only the sense is given in the base and whose reference is determined by a rule of semantic interpretation which, he claims, operates after the operation of certain syntactic transformations. The meaning of these noun phrases can, on this analysis, not be determined in the base but only after the appropriate rules of semantic interpretation have assigned reference. The rules that precede the assignment of reference may well affect the meaning of the sentence by altering the structure to which the rules of semantic interpretation apply.

Irrespective of differences, the assumption that reflexives and their antecedents have the same reference is a part of almost every formulation of the transformational theory of reflexivization. Gleitman (1965), however, has in a footnote (n.26) questioned the validity of this assumption. In support of her objection she offers for consideration the sentence given in (6).

(6) Organisms reproduce themselves

She does not spell out her understanding of this sentence, but she might have had in mind considerations such as these. It is surely not possible for any given organism to yield itself by the process of reproduction. In the same sense it is not possible for all organisms to yield themselves, each its own self, by the process of reproduction. Hence, this can not be the meaning of sentence (6). One might then go on to conclude that the meaning of (6) is that each organism (or pair of organisms) yields another by the process of reproduction and that the reference of the reflexive can not be the same as that of its antecedent, though its sense might be. But a one to one pairing of reproducing and reproduced organisms is not the only and, indeed, not the proper interpretation of the meaning of sentence (6). Rather, the meaning of this sentence is that the set of organisms taken as a whole yields itself by the process of reproduction. On this interpretation, the noun phrase <u>organisms</u> refers to the set of organisms just as the reflexive <u>themselves</u> refers to the set of organisms. Both the reflexive and its antecedent have the same reference.

Another sentence that, like (6), could be analyzed as counter-evidence to the claim that reflexives and their antecedents have the same reference is given in (7).

(7) History repeats itself

If one interprets the noun phrase history, the antecedent of the reflexive itself, too narrowly so that it refers to specific historical events, then sentence (7) would be untrue. Knowing it to be true, however, one might contend that this is so because the reflexive and its antecedent do not refer to the same specific historical events and hence do not have the same reference. To impose such an interpretation on this sentence would force one to give the verb repeat a meaning which it does not ordinarily have. Repeated events do not normally differ. If the noun phrase <u>history</u> is repeated more broadly, however, so that it refers to the pattern of historical events rather than to the events themselves, then the interpretation of sentence (7) is straightforward. The pattern of events referred to by the subject noun phrase is the same as the pattern of events referred to by the reflexive object of the sentence.

Sentences (6) and (7) do not represent a serious challenge to the validity of the assumption that reflexives and their antecedents have the same reference, and it is fair to accept this assumption as valid. In this point both the transformational and the phrase structure theory of reflexivization agree. The transformational theory, however, also assumes that reflexives and their antecedents have the same sense. It has already been shown earlier that two noun phrases may have the same reference and yet not have the same sense. Hence, one can accept the assumption that reflexives and their antecedents have the same reference without accepting the assumption that reflexives and their antecedents have the same sense, a possibility that the transformational theory of reflexivization completely ignores.

Precisely this is what the phrase structure theory of reflexives does. It does not challenge the validity of the contention that reflexives and their antecedents have the same reference, though it does challenge the validity of the assumption that reflexives and their antecedents have the same sense. Reflexives, on the assumptions of this theory, are analyzed as restricted possessives with the head noun self and bound anaphoric pronouns as determiners. Their reference is accounted for by the following simple rule: A reflexive has the same reference as the antecedent of its determiner. Their sense is a function of the sense of their head and the sense of their determiners. The head noun, however, is always the same. Therefore, the sense of the head noun is fixed. It does not vary with the particular antecedent noun phrase that the reflexive is associated with, as it does in the transformational theory of reflexivization.

It is not easy, if it is indeed possible, directly to

specify the sense of reflexives taken as a whole, but one can approach this question in an indirect way. It was noted earlier that it is possible for two noun phrases having the same reference not to have the same sense, but that it is not possible for two noun phrases having the same reference to be of opposite sense. With the understanding that the term feature is used to refer to the criteria in the statement of the sense of a noun or noun phrase, this can be recast in the following terms. A noun phrase that has the same reference as some other noun phrase may not be marked positively for a feature for which the other is marked negatively or negatively for a feature for which the other is marked positively. It is, of course, possible for a noun phrase that has the same reference as some other noun phrase to be unmarked for a feature for which the other is marked. Reflexives in particular may not be marked positively or negatively for a feature for which one of their possible antecedents is marked the opposite way, negatively or positively, respectively. Since any noun phrase is a possible antecedent of an appropriate reflexive, reflexives as a whole may not be marked for a feature for which some noun phrase is marked the opposite way. As a consequence, reflexives must be highly unmarked. Since reflexives

are marked for few if any features there are few if any
criteria that an object must satisfy in order for a reflexive
to apply to it. There is nothing in the statement of the
sense of reflexives that might distinguish objects to which
they apply from objects to which they might not apply.

Since reflexives and their antecedents are not identical
in feature composition, it follows that they do not have the
same meaning. In general, the meaning of a sentence, insofar
as it does not involve idiomatic expressions, is a compositional
function of the meaning of its constituents. In view of this
any two sentences that do not differ with respect to the
meanings of their constituents should not differ in meaning.
Consider, for instance, the sentence given in example (8).

(8) Only the devil pities himself

The meaning of sentence (8) is a compositional function of the
meaning of its constituents. If one substitutes for any of the
constituents of (8) other appropriate forms that have the same
meaning, the meaning of this sentence is not changed. If, for
instance, one substitutes for the noun phrase the devil in the
subject of (8) the noun phrase Satan one obtains the sentence
Only Satan pities himself. This sentence does indeed have the
same meaning as sentence (8). By the same token, if one

substitutes for the verb _pities_ the verb _has pity for_, one obtains the sentence _Only the devil has pity for himself_. This sentence again has the same meaning as sentence (8). Now if reflexives have the same meaning as their antecedents, as the transformational theory of reflexivization assumes, then if substituting for the reflexive a copy of its antecedent yields a viable sentence, one would expect the meaning of this sentence to be the same as the meaning of sentence (8). If, as the phrase structure theory of reflexives assumes, reflexives do not have the same meaning as their antecedents, then one would not necessarily expect the resultant sentence to have the same meaning as sentence (8). In the case of example (8) substituting a copy of the antecedent of the reflexive for the reflexive itself, does yield a viable sentence. This sentence is given in (9).

(9) Only the devil pities the devil

The meaning of this sentence is not the same as the meaning of sentence (8), contrary to the prediction of the transformational theory of reflexivization. In particular, while sentence (8) could be true if the devil is not the only one who pities the devil, sentence (9) would not.

This then shows that the assumption that reflexives and

their antecedents have the same meaning is false, it is nevertheless true that reflexives and their antecedents have the same reference. They differ only with regard to the criteria by which they identify the object of their reference. This fact is captured by the phrase structure theory of reflexives, where reflexives do not have the same meaning as the antecedent noun phrases they are associated with. The transformational theory of reflexivization, on the other hand, conflicts with this fact since this theory contends that reflexives and their antecedents have the same meaning.

BIBLIOGRAPHY

Bresnan, Joan W. (1970) "On Complementizers: Toward a Syntactic Theory of Complement Types," Cambridge, Mass.: The Computation Laboratory of Harvard University, Report No. NSF-24.

Browne, E. Wayles (1967) "On the Problem of Enclitic Placement in Serbo-Croatian," unpublished paper.

Chomsky, Noam (1965) Aspects of the Theory of Syntax. Cambridge, Mass.: MIT Press.

_____ (1967=1970) "Remarks on Nominalizations," in Roderick A. Jacobs and Peter S. Rosenbaum (eds.), Readings in English Transformational Grammar. Waltham, Mass.: Blaisdell Publishing Co.

_____ (1968=1970) "Deep Structure, Surface Structure, and Semantic Interpretation," in Roman Jakobson and Shigeo Kawamoto (eds.), Studies in General and Oriental Linguistics. Tokyo: TEC Co., pp. 52-91.

Dougherty, Ray C. (1968) A Transformational Grammar of Co-ordinate Conjoined Structures. Cambridge, Mass.: MIT doctoral dissertation.

Emonds, Joseph E. (1970) Root and Structure-Preserving Transformations. Cambridge, Mass.: MIT doctoral dissertation.

Frege, Gottlob (1892) "Über Sinn and Bedeutung," Zeitschrift fur Philosophie und Philosophische Kritik 100.25-50.

Gleitman, Lila R. (1965) "Coordinating Conjunctions in English," Language 41.260-293.

Hall, Barbara C. (1965) Subject and Object in Modern English. Cambridge, Mass.: MIT doctoral dissertation.

Halle, Morris (1964a) formal discussion of Postal (1964a), in Horace G. Lunt (ed.), Proceedings of the Ninth International Congress of Linguists. The Hague: Mouton and Co., pp. 356-357.

Halle, Morris (1964b) "Some Rules of Language," *The Technology Review* vol. 67, December 1964, pp. 37-38.

Jackendoff, Ray S. (1969a) "An Interpretive Theory of Pronouns and Reflexives," Washington, D.C.: Center for Applied Linguistics, PEGS paper No. 27.

_____ (1969b) *Some Rules of Semantic Interpretation for English*. Cambridge, Mass.: MIT doctoral dissertation.

Kayne, Richard S. (1969) *The Transformational Cycle in French Syntax*. Cambridge, Mass.: MIT doctoral dissertation.

Keyser, S. Jay (1964) "Our Manner of Speaking," *The Technology Review* vol. 66, February 1964, pp. 19-21.

_____ and Morris Halle (1968) "What Do We Do When We Speak," in Paul A. Kolers and Murray Eden (eds.), *Recognizing Patterns: Studies in Living and Automatic Systems*. Cambridge, Mass.: MIT Press, pp. 63-80.

Langacker, Ronald W. (1966=1969) "On Pronominalization and the Chain of Command," in David A. Reibel and Sanford A. Schane (eds.), *Modern Studies in English: Readings in Transformational Grammar*. Englewood Cliffs, N.J.: Prentice Hall, pp. 160-186.

Lees, Robert B. and Edward S. Klima (1963) "Rules for English Pronominalization," *Language* 39. 17-29.

Perlmutter, David M. (1968) *Deep and Surface Constraints in Syntax*. Cambridge, Mass.: MIT doctoral dissertation.

Postal, Paul M. (1962) *Some Syntactic Rules in Mohawk*. New Haven, Conn.: Yale University doctoral dissertation.

_____ (1964a) "Mohawk Prefix Generation," in Horace G. Lunt (ed.), *Proceedings of the Ninth International Congress of Linguists*. The Hague: Mouton and Co., pp. 346-355.

_____ (1964b) "Underlying and Superficial Linguistic Structure," *Harvard Educational Review* 34. 246-266.

Postal, Paul M. (1966a) "A Note on 'Understood Transitively'," *International Journal of American Linguistics* 32. 90-93.

_____ (1966b) "On So-Called Pronouns in English," in Francis P. Dinneen, S.J. (ed.), *Monograph Series on Language and Linguistics No. 19*. Washington, D.C.: Georgetown University Press, pp. 177-206.

_____ (1968a) "Cross-Over Phenomena," in Warren J. Plath (ed.), *Specification and Utilization of a Transformational Grammar, Scientific Report No. 3. AFCRL-68-0371*. Yorktown Heights, N.Y.: IBM Watson Research Center.

_____ (1968b) "On Coreferential Complement Subject Deletion," Yorktown Heights, N.Y.: IBM Watson Research Center, Report No. RC 2252.

Quang Phuc Dong (1967) "English Sentences without Overt Grammatical Subject," unpublished paper.

Rosenbaum, Peter S. (1965) "A Principle Governing Deletion in English Sentential Complementation," Yorktown Heights, N.Y.: IBM Watson Research Center, Report No. RC 1519.

_____ (1967) *The Grammar of English Predicate Complement Constructions*. Cambridge, Mass.: MIT Press.

Ross, John Robert (1967) *Constraints on Variables in Syntax*. Cambridge, Mass.: MIT doctoral dissertation.

_____ (1968=1970) "On Declarative Sentences," in Roderick A. Jacobs and Peter S. Rosenbaum (eds.), *Readings in English Transformational Grammar*. Waltham, Mass.: Blaisdell Publishing Co.

Strang, Barbara M.H. (1962) *Modern English Structure*. London: Edward Arnold Publishers.